מאורי השנה

Power Lines

מאורי השנה

Power Lines

*Insights and Reflections
on the Jewish Holidays*

Ephraim Nisenbaum

TARGUM/FELDHEIM

First published 2002
Copyright © 2002 by Ephraim Nisenbaum
ISBN 1-56871-229-4

All rights reserved

No part of this publication may be translated, reproduced, stored in a retrieval system, or transmitted in any form or by any means, electronic, mechanical, photocopying, recording, or otherwise, without prior permission in writing from both the copyright holder and the publisher.

Published by:
TARGUM PRESS, INC.
22700 W. Eleven Mile Rd.
Southfield, MI 48034
E-mail: targum@netvision.net.il
Fax: 888-298-9992
www.targum.com

Distributed by:
FELDHEIM PUBLISHERS
202 Airport Executive Park
Nanuet, NY 10954
www.feldheim.com

Printed in Israel

Comments may be directed to the author at enisenbaum@aol.com

אברהם חיים לוין
RABBI AVROHOM CHAIM LEVIN
5104 N. DRAKE AVENUE • CHICAGO, IL 60625
ROSH HAYESHIVA/TELSHE-CHICAGO • ראש הישיבה/טלז-שיקגו

ב"ה

יום א' לסדר ולא תחנפו

ידידי הרב הג' ר' אברהם ניסן דוד שליט"א

הנה מתחילת השנה שאנו נואמנו, וכבר
כמה אנשי אמונה רד שטריקל רמ"ד ואלופי
הגאון כדור קליוולנד ויד"נ כ"ש בריו דלן
אמור עברו בהתעצ' לאמתתא דהאי
ודבר דעלית לגבי' ספר על הארבע
רועות הקלעסיע ותהא אלווית דברי
מנוחה והדרכה ירואת אנשים והרבה
ובכל דף עקבות וציורי התוצרת כו
כתר חיפוץ בהבנות דברי הזמן ונמצאת
ודברים יקרים הדרבנה ישלו ...
ונתברך וניכוב התזמור להאיר אורם מצל
להפיץ על הרבים ואשר לעזל וחזו וחקל
אהבתם תש הלוי וין ידידו האהוב ודבוק

OFFICE: 3535 W. FOSTER AVENUE • CHICAGO, IL 60625 • 312/463-7738 • FAX 312/463-2849

בס"ד

שמואל קמנצקי
Rabbi S. Kamenetsky

Study: 215-473-1212
Home: 215-473-2798

2018 Upland Way
Philadelphia, Pa 19131

August 7, 2002

Rabbi Ephraim Nisenbaum
2362 Milton
University Heights, OH 44118

Dear Rabbi Nisenbaum, שליט"א

"Power Lines" is a well-written review of the highlights of the Jewish calendar. It emphasizes the significance and beauty of the special days of the year.

Your book is enhanced by the midrashim and מאמרי חז"ל which you include, as well as the divrei Torah of the gedolei Yisroel of our times. The meshalim you use to clarify many ideas broaden our comprehension. The interesting facts and customs you present so clearly will benefit readers of all ages. It makes learning a pleasurable experience.

May you be זוכה to be among the מצדיקי הרבים.

Sincerely Yours,

Rabbi Shmuel Kamenetsky

Vaad L'Hatzolas Nidchei Yisroel

of Stam Gemilas Chesed Fund, Inc.   Tax Exempt #22-2371275
401 Yeshiva Lane • Baltimore, Maryland 21208 • Tel: 410-484-7396
Fax: 410-486-8810 • E-Mail: eisemann@juno.com

Rabbi Moshe M. Eisemann

May 28, 2002

Rabbi Ephraim Nisenbaum
2362 Milton
University Heights, OH 44118

Dear R' Ephraim:

As soon as I saw your latest book, this time on the Yomim Tovim, I knew that it would be energized by a great deal of creative thinking. It would serve as a challenge to all of us to embark on our own journey of discovery. I believe that a challenge to find the new, the as yet untested, is just what we need in a book of this kind. My own experience tells me that it is easy enough to have familiarity breed complacency and superficiality.

Your easy-to-read essays fill a void that needs filling. We are blessed with many *Sefarim* [though most of these are in Hebrew] which breathe life into these wonderful days. However, they do this at the interface between *niglah* and *nistar* and many of us are not yet ready to deal with such profound ideas. Your thoughts are easy to handle. They make the transition between a theoretical appreciation and a more practical application smooth and inviting.

The "Power Lines" of your title are particularly suggestive, beyond the metaphor for which you use them in your interesting Introduction. Power lines carry electricity to us, they help to shed light and to warm, in short, to make a house into a home. However, we have to throw the switch. If we don't, the energy remains outside – useless.

I suspect that all your readers will be able to make their own way from *mashal* to *nimshal* here.

Best wishes and thanks for sharing all this with us.

Moshe M. Eisemann

In loving memory of

Naomi Blair Comet

נחמה בת הרב משה

Her deep love of Torah,
Israel, family, and the Jewish people
is sorely missed.

In loving memory of

Philip A. Arian
אברהם פסח בן בנימין

Whose kindness and love of family
continue to resonate through the generations.

Kathy and Robert Leb
and family

Contents

Acknowledgments 13
Introduction 17

Rosh Hashanah

High Holiday Preparations 23
The Selichos Connection 26
Rosh Hashanah and the Oral Torah 29
Malchiyos, Zichronos, and Shofaros 33
Capture the Moment 36
Shofar, Shabbos, and Me 39
The Joyous Awe of Rosh Hashanah 45

Yom Kippur

The Happiest Day of the Year 51
Holy, Holy, Holy 56
Yom Kippur and the Yetzer Hara 60

Sukkos

The Joy of Life 65
Fulfilling the Will of Hashem 69
Circles of Significance 74
The Atonement of Sukkos 78

Hoshana Rabbah, Shemini Atzeres, and Simchas Torah

Prayers for Rain 83
Victors in Judgment 86
The Simchah and the Torah 88

Chanukah

Chanukah and the Secret of Beginnings 93
Reflection on the Last Day of Chanukah 101
The Dreidel and Hashem's Chanukah Presence . . . 107
Between Darkness and Light 111
The Victory Over Reason 114
Internal Influence 117

Tu B'Shevat

Teachings of the Trees 123
The Mitzvos of Eretz Yisrael 126

Purim

Finding the Happy Medium 133
A Month of Joy 137
The Torah of Purim 140
Amalek and the Power of Lishmah 144
Purim and Seeing beyond Self 148

The Four Parshiyos

Parashas Shekalim: United We Stand 155
Parashas Zachor: Amalek and the Danger of Doubt . . 158
Parashas Parah: The Atonement beyond Understanding . . 164
Parashas Hachodesh: The Gift of Time 168

Pesach

An Educated Freedom 173
The Taste of Haste 176

The Right Appetite	180
The Ultimate Victory	184
The Miracle of the Sea	187
Expecting the Unexpected	191

Sefiras Ha'omer and Lag Ba'omer

Making Days Count	197
A Life of Torah	203

Shavuos

A Time for Torah; a Torah for All Time	209
The Wedding Season	212
The Power of a Commitment	215
The Antidote	219
A Torah of Chesed	222

Tishah B'Av

Tishah B'Av and the Fast Days	229
The Limitations of Mourning	232
Mourning the Loss of Reality	235
The Yom Tov of Tishah B'Av	239
The Art of Loving Every Jew	242
Tu B'Av: Repairing the Destruction	252

Shabbos

The Day of the Inner Dimension	259
Candle Lighting and Chava	263
Shabbos and the Mishkan	266
The Shabbos Family	270

Glossary	275

Acknowledgments

אודה ה' מאד בפי ובתוך רבים אהללנו.

"I will thank Hashem exceedingly with my mouth; amid the many I will praise Him."

(Tehillim 109:30)

Appreciation must be expressed in the proper forum. The more we recognize Hashem's kindness to us, the more of an obligation we have to express our gratitude to Him. It is interesting to note that the Hebrew phrase for appreciation is *hakaras hatov*, the recognition of goodness or kindness. This is because it is impossible to properly appreciate a kindness until it is clearly recognized.

It is difficult to even begin thanking Hashem for everything He has given me until this day, allowing me to publish my second book of Torah insights. I am most fortunate for my parents, Reb Ya'akov and Karen Nisenbaum, שיחיו לאיי״ט, for whom no sacrifice is ever too great for the sake of the *chinuch* of their children. My siblings and I are blessed to have them as role models in *ahavas Torah*, *chesed*, and humility. May *HaKadosh Baruch Hu* grant them the merit to enjoy *nachas* from all their children and grandchildren for many years to come.

My appreciation is also due my in-laws, Rabbi Chaim Tzvi and Gittel Goldzweig, שליט״א, who have always helped us in so many ways. They are truly paradigms of *ahavas Torah, mesirus nefesh,* and *chesed,* worthy bearers of their holy legacies. May they enjoy much *nachas* from the whole family for many years.

I am appreciative for the *hadrachah* (guidance) and *chinuch* I received from all my rebbeim: from the foundations at the Hebrew Academy of Cleveland and Telshe Yeshiva in Cleveland, to the nurturing and *derech halimud* I received from my *roshei yeshivah* in Telshe Yeshiva, Chicago — HaRav Avrohom Chaim Levin, שליט״א, HaRav Chaim Dov Keller, שליט״א, and להבחל״ח HaRav Chaim Schmelczer, זצ״ל. I have also been very fortunate to benefit from the wisdom and *hadrachah* of the esteemed *mashgiach,* HaRav Shlomo Wolbe, שליט״א. My family has also had the good fortune of benefiting from the friendship and wisdom of the Clevelander-Nadvorner Rebbe, presently in Ra'anana, Israel, HaRav Isaac Rosenbaum, שליט״א.

Thank you to my good *chaverim* who reviewed much of the material in this *sefer* and offered constructive comments: Rabbis Yitzchak Miller, Sruly Koval, Shmuel Schmelczer, and my brother-in-law, Rabbi Moshe Aharon Levinson. My good friends Sam Harris, Dr. William Wieder, and Dr. Moshe Harris also reviewed parts of the manuscript. My gratitude to them all, and may Hashem repay their kindness many times over.

Most of the material in this book has been presented to my students in the Jewish Learning Connection. They have challenged me and forced me to think, re-think, and clarify the material over and over again. I am privileged to be able to spend my days serving those who thirst for the truth of Torah.

Some of these essays have been presented in classes and lectures I have given at Beis Yaakov of Mosdos Ohr HaTorah. I appreciate the opportunity to share these insights with young

Acknowledgments

women who exhibit such a genuine thirst, appreciation, and enthusiasm for Torah.

I am fortunate to have been blessed with children, שיחיו, who have always shown an interest in, and have served as sounding boards for, many of the ideas presented.

I am grateful to Mr. Harold Males, Ms. Jill Brotman, Mrs. Chaya Newman, along with Mrs. Ita Olesker and the staff at Targum Press, for lending their expertise to the manuscript, truly creating a masterpiece from my feeble efforts. Mrs. Esther Goodman, Mrs. Pesie Dewick, and my daughter Malkie assisted with proofreading. My appreciation to Mrs. Ellen Wohl for suggesting the title. Thank you also to Rabbi Moshe Dombey for taking an interest in this *sefer*.

This work would never have materialized without the constant encouragement and selflessness of my dear wife Chanie, שתחי׳. Her gentle influence is keenly felt in anything and everything I have been fortunate enough to accomplish. May we both be deserving of Hashem's blessings for many years to come, and see our children grow to become great in Torah and in the service of Hashem.

Introduction

When we think of holidays, we usually picture images of relaxation and vacations. But whereas these images may be appropriate to secular life, they do not portray the Jewish holidays. The Jewish holidays do not spare us work.

Anyone who has been involved in the gut-wrenching *teshuvah* (repentance) of the High Holidays, or in the meticulous choosing of a beautiful *esrog* and the construction of a sukkah for Sukkos, knows that Jewish holidays are no vacation. The painstaking scrubbing and cleaning of the house and the harried experience of baking matzos for Pesach are not relaxing; nor is studying Torah through the night of Shavuos a vacation from "work." A Jewish holiday matches the original meaning of the word and contains holiness. We are offered the opportunity to grow spiritually and connect to Hashem.

Each holiday has a unique theme and special observances. When we observe the details properly, we may aspire to greater heights throughout the year. For example, the message of Rosh Hashanah is renewal, the ability to start over. The theme of Yom Kippur is forgiveness. That of Sukkos is *simchah* and joy. Pesach is freedom and independence. Shavuos is a renewed connection to Torah. When a person approaches Rosh Hashanah with the right attitude and strives to observe all of the details of the day's mitzvos, he will feel a sense of freshness and renewal. Sukkos will bring an added sense of joy and tranquility. Each of the holidays, properly observed, similarly enriches our lives.

The title of this book is based on an analogy I once heard comparing the Jewish holidays to electric power-line poles. Power lines run from one pole to the next, but they are not taut. The wires, in fact, meet the poles at their highest point. From there, they slowly descend to the midpoints between the poles. Then, the wires climb higher and higher, until they reach the next poles — again the highest point.

Think of ordinary days as the sloping power lines, and the holidays as their high points. Just as the poles are the point at which the wires have the greatest tension, the holidays provide a boost, a time when the Jew's batteries are recharged and his spirits soar to a peak. After the holidays pass, spirits tend to sag, until the mid-point between the two holidays. Then spirits ascend once again, in preparation for the next holiday — the next boost.

But before we can be recharged by the holidays, we must first understand the unique nature of each. We must open ourselves to each holiday's special character. This requires an investment of time and effort. The more we are willing to prepare, the more we will benefit.

In this collection of essays, I have tried to examine the various holidays, their names, and their special mitzvos. I have aimed for a straightforward description that is, hopefully, easy to follow. Although the presentation may be new, the material is all based on principles learned from my *rebbeim* or gathered from the works of the Baalei Mussar and Chassidic masters. The essays vary in length and character: some long, some short; some inspirational, others educational. I hope this work makes possible a deeper appreciation of each of the holidays. If, in some small way, this collection of essays helps "boost" the reader to experience the Jewish holidays in a more mature and spiritual manner, my goal will have been realized.[1]

---

1 In keeping with the opinion of the Rokeach that an author's name be hinted in the title, the Hebrew title of the book, מאורי השנה, has the same numerical value (617) as the author's name, אפרים נחום, with that of his father, יעקב.

Rosh Hashanah

High Holiday Preparations

A medical examination provides a lesson on how to prepare for and better appreciate the Holidays

Several years ago, a friend showed me an article from *Life* magazine (September, 1996) entitled "Portraits of a People." In describing Rosh Hashanah, the author, Charles Hirshberg, tells us:

> Several million Americans will undergo a spectacular transformation...chanting beautiful ancient blessings as candles flicker.... [They will] share loaves of sweet, amber bread and apples dipped in honey..., enter tabernacles where white-robed cantors sing the praises of the Lord...[and] embrace one another and offer traditional greetings.... [They will also] walk to a stream or lake and cast crumbs of bread upon the water, a symbol of their wish to cleanse themselves of selfishness and sin.

The superficiality of this presentation of Judaism troubled me. Is this how Judaism is perceived on the street? And worse, by other Jews? How can the essence of the Jewish New Year be captured by blessings and greetings, by apples and honey, and by bread crumbs cast upon the water? Is it these activities that create the "spectacular transformation"? In fact, Mr. Hirshberg never even refers to the High Holidays as "days of awe."

Rosh Hashanah is the day of judgment, when life and death issues are decided and man's destiny is determined; yet *teshuvah*, fear, and prayer seem to play no role in Mr. Hirshberg's overall Rosh Hashanah scheme. And I suspect he is not alone in his painfully shallow understanding of this important day!

How are we to approach Rosh Hashanah in order to gain the proper appreciation of its importance in the Jewish year? I recently had an experience that gave me a better understanding and helped me put things in perspective. I had been experiencing abdominal problems, and my physician ordered a comprehensive internal exam. A number of rigorous procedures, some quite uncomfortable, were required to prepare my "innards" for the gastrointestinal work-up. The preparations contributed to the fear and anxiety I was already experiencing. Suffice it to say that my regular prayers on the day of the exam took on a new seriousness and urgency.

Ultimately, when the examination showed nothing seriously wrong, I felt a wave of relief and joy. It was as if a heavy load had been removed from my back. It struck me that the whole experience was a model for the High Holiday season.

Before the High Holidays arrive, we must also go through a "prep period" to rid ourselves of the undesirable matter that clogs our souls. This is done during the month of Elul and, more specifically, during the days of *selichos*, through *teshuvah*, and by increasing our prayers. Only after these preparations are we ready for the judgment, when Hashem examines each person thoroughly, assessing his or her actions, and makes His decision. Without proper preparation, it is impossible to appreciate or experience the essence of Rosh Hashanah. The Day of Judgment is reduced to a day for dipping apples in honey.

The analogy to the medical exam, however, is not totally accurate. The cleansing prior to the medical exam enables the doctor to make a determination, but has no bearing on the actual condition — nor on the prospects for the future.

For Rosh Hashanah, however, the cleansing itself affects the outcome, positively influencing Hashem's judgment. With thorough preparation, we can hope to be judged favorably and granted a sweet new year. Only then do our greetings, the dipping of apples in honey, and the emptying of our pockets into streams take on meaning, as symbols of our eternal optimism. If the prior preparation is not taken seriously, such optimism is baseless. Without preparation, the symbols are empty.

Taking the analogy a bit further, the medical examination primarily assesses the patient's present state of health. If we have an eye to the future, we must follow the doctor's advice to maintain a healthy diet and active lifestyle. Similarly, a serious Rosh Hashanah preparation must include a commitment for the future, to continue to observe the Great Doctor's instructions for physical and spiritual good health. Then we can hope we will be worthy of receiving Hashem's blessings for the upcoming year. May we all merit a clean bill of health!

The Selichos Connection

Two explanations for early rising for prayer before Rosh Hashanah

In the days before Rosh Hashanah, Jews rise earlier than usual to recite special *selichos* prayers and supplications, in preparation for the Days of Awe. Ashkenazic Jews customarily begin *selichos* on *motza'ei Shabbos* (Saturday night) after midnight. *Selichos* are said at least four consecutive days before Rosh Hashanah begins, and so they begin either one or two Saturday evenings before the start of the High Holidays. Sephardic Jews begin *selichos* with the start of the month of Elul.

Why did the Rabbis deem the recital of special prayers at an earlier-than-usual time of day, more than any other mitzvah, as a way of preparing for the judgment of Rosh Hashanah?

A recurring theme throughout the High Holiday service is the *akeidas Yitzchak*. This is the test given our forefather Avraham by Hashem, to see if he would offer up his only son Yitzchak as a sacrifice on the *mizbe'ach*. Each day a section of the *selichos* prayers recalls the *akeidah*, when Avraham's selfless love for

Hashem was demonstrated by his willingness to sacrifice his beloved son. This is an integral part of the Jewish heritage. We recall Avraham's merit as we ask for assistance in our judgment at the start of each new year.

Avraham's response to Hashem's instructions is a model for us on many levels. His enthusiasm is one of them. As the Torah relates, "Avraham woke early in the morning and saddled his donkey... [Then he] went to the place of which Hashem had spoken to him" (*Bereishis* 22:3). We can only imagine the difficulty of Avraham's task, yet he enthusiastically fulfilled Hashem's will by rising early.

The Talmud (*Pesachim* 4a) understands from this passage that all mitzvos should be fulfilled similarly — without delay and with zeal. Thus, the motivation for reciting *selichos* prayers early in the morning may have a dual source: not only to share the merit of the *akeidah* itself, but also the merit of Avraham's enthusiasm. But perhaps we can provide another reason for rising early, as well.

The Chafetz Chaim, Rabbi Yisrael Meir Kagan (1838–1933), began rising earlier in his later years. When asked to explain his behavior, he responded:

> I know that at my advanced age I do not have many more years to live. When my time comes, I know I will be called before the Heavenly Tribunal in judgment. I do not know how they will judge me, but I imagine that they will take out a volume of *Shulchan Aruch* (*The Code of Jewish Law*) and examine my observance of each halachah. The first halachah in *Shulchan Aruch* discusses how a person must get out of bed early in the morning, like a lion, in order to fulfill the mitzvos of Hashem. How would it look if I cannot answer

the first question properly? What an embarrassment! For this reason, I have started rising earlier to pray each day. At least that way I will spare myself the shame of not responding properly to the first question.

Perhaps the judgment that occurs on Rosh Hashanah is similar. Hashem judges each person, following the order of the halachos in the *Shulchan Aruch*. How will it look if we cannot answer the first question properly? Accordingly we prepare for the High Holidays by rising earlier than usual and reciting *selichos*.

Rosh Hashanah and the Oral Torah

The significance of the Oral Torah to the Jewish New Year, the history of humankind, and the mitzvos

Rosh Hashanah is associated with being the beginning of the Jewish New Year, but it is also the Day of Judgment for all mankind. Remarkably, though, the Torah does not say that Rosh Hashanah marks a new calendar year or signals an annual day of judgment. The name "Rosh Hashanah" isn't even found in Scripture. The Torah only refers to "the first day of the seventh month...a day of sounding the trumpets" (*Bamidbar* 29:1) — a description hardly evocative of a new year[1] or the time of Hashem's judgment.

Rosh Hashanah, as the beginning of the year and as a time of judgment, is based on a rabbinic tradition in the Talmud. The Rabbis determined the date of Creation[2] and understood that

---

1 The seventh month is calculated from the month of Nissan, the month marking the birth of the Jewish nation after the Exodus from Egypt. Rosh Hashanah marks the anniversary of Creation.
2 See Talmud (*Rosh Hashanah* 12a). See also Maharal, *Chidushei*

this day would be a propitious time for Hashem's judgment of each individual. Accordingly, they prepared various prayers and customs for the day. Yet the question begs clarification. Why was so important a day scanted in the Torah, and relegated to the Talmud to have both its essence defined and its requirements spelled out?

Basic Jewish belief requires that we accept not only the Written Torah, but also the Oral Torah that was taught to Moshe by Hashem. The need for an Oral Torah is evident after even a superficial study of the Written Torah, which appears to be incomplete. Many of the mitzvos are written so ambiguously that it is impossible to understand their requirements. The details of important mitzvos, such as the binding of tefillin and the performance of ritual slaughter, are barely mentioned in the Written Torah. Other passages seem to contradict each other. This absence of detail appears to negate the very purpose of the Torah: to serve as a guidebook for service to Hashem.

The Oral Torah given to Moshe is essential as a supplement to the Written Torah. It was transmitted by Moshe to Yehoshua to the judges and prophets, and so on, from one generation to the next. Eventually, after almost two thousand years, these details were recorded in the Talmud.

The Oral Torah serves two functions: First, it fills in the details for many of the mitzvos not explained in the Torah. Second, it provides a set of divinely ordained principles by which the Torah can be properly interpreted. These principles make it possible to apply the Torah to any set of circumstances or situations — even those that arise in contemporary times. The Talmud derives many details and laws by applying the thirteen hermeneutic prin-

---

Aggados Rosh Hashanah 10b, for further explanation.

ciples. However, the Oral Torah also includes ordinances and "fences" of Rabbinic origin. The purpose of these are to advance and improve religious observance and to prevent transgression.

The Oral Torah is not mere theory or interpretation. It is the essence of Jewish belief and practice; without it, the Torah cannot be observed or even understood. Rav Shlomo Wolbe once remarked that the sanctity of our Shabbos observance stems more from the Talmudic tractate of *Shabbos* than it does from the Scriptural passages relating to Shabbos.[3]

The centrality of the oral interpretation and rabbinic ordinances can be seen from the very first mitzvah in the Torah: the commandment forbidding Adam to eat from the *eitz hada'as*, the Tree of Knowledge. Hashem ordered Adam not to eat from the tree. When Adam relayed the prohibition to Chava, though, he added a protective fence — an additional stricture — that they must not even touch the tree. When the serpent enticed Chava and she touched the tree, she did not die, as touching the tree was not part of Hashem's commandment. The serpent then told Chava that just as she had not died from touching the tree, she would not die from eating its fruit. Chava accepted the serpent's argument, ate, and gave some to Adam to eat as well. The Rabbis (*Sanhedrin* 29a) actually fault Adam for having added to the prohibition, as this led them to sin. Adam had failed to distinguish between Hashem's prohibition and his own addition. But Adam's recognition of the need for a fence around the only mitzvah given to him says much about the need for rabbinic ordinances.

A similar idea can be seen in the very first section of the Talmud. The mishnah in *Berachos* (2a) discusses the time for saying

---

3   I heard this from Rav Wolbe in a *va'ad* at *Be'er Ya'akov*, 5739.

the Shema. The Rabbis' opinion is that the nighttime Shema can be said until midnight. Rabban Gamliel disagrees, saying the Shema can be said until dawn. Rabban Gamliel then adds that, in truth, even the Rabbis agree that the Shema can be said until dawn; yet, concerned that a person might fall asleep and fail to say the Shema, they created a fence and ruled it must be said by midnight.

Here, too, the Talmud shows us, at the beginning of its first discussion of any mitzvah, the necessity of rabbinic involvement in Torah observance.

We can now explain why the main thrust of Rosh Hashanah is not mentioned in Scripture. Our basic understanding of the ways in which Hashem judges, rewards, and punishes man is based on an oral tradition. Explanations of such fundamental concepts as the World to Come and Heaven and Hell are not found in the Written Torah. Similarly, the nature of our judgment on Rosh Hashanah is based on rabbinic tradition. Perhaps Hashem hid the essence of the very first day of the year — the day that defines our faith and relationship with the Creator — within the oral tradition to foster our appreciation of the important role of oral law.

The Jewish year opens with a holiday requiring rabbinic interpretation and input if we are to understand its essence. In other words, only through a thorough study of the Talmud and the oral law can we begin to appreciate the ABC's of Judaism.

Malchiyos, Zichronos, and Shofaros

The three parts of Musaf are linked to Hashem's concern for three types of sin

The Torah calls Rosh Hashanah "*Yom Teruah*," the Day of Shofar Blasts. In trying to determine what sound it is that must be produced by the shofar, the Talmud (*Rosh Hashanah* 32b) teaches that the word *teruah* means "a broken, wailing cry." The Talmud proves this from the Aramaic translation of the word *teruah*, "*yabava*," the same word used in the Prophets (*Shoftim* 5:28) for the broken groans uttered by the mother of the wicked general Sisera when he failed to return from battle with the Children of Israel.

It must be explained why the details of so great a mitzvah as shofar are derived from an incident involving so wicked a character as Sisera's mother. After all, this was a heartless woman who eagerly awaited her son's return from a bloody war with plunder, with beautiful gifts for her. Is there some kind of connection between Sisera's mother and the sounding of the shofar?

We can clarify this by examining the Musaf prayers of Rosh

Hashanah, which satisfy three requirements: "Say before Me *malchiyos* (passages of rulership) that you may accept My rule upon you; *zichronos* (passages of remembrance, most specifically the *akeidas Yitzchak*) in order that I may remember you favorably; and how so? Through *shofaros* (sounding of the shofar)" (*Rosh Hashanah* 16a). What is the significance of these three topics and their connection to Rosh Hashanah?

It is possible that these three subjects remind us of the three sins that remove a person from the world: jealousy, lust, and arrogance (*Avos* 4:21). These three sins are also the root cause of all other sins.[4] Jealousy is the source of sins of emotion; lust is the source of bodily sins; and arrogance (as well as the pursuit of honor) is the source of intellectual sins.[5] With the recital of the passages of *malchiyos*, we intellectually accept upon ourselves the yoke of Hashem's rule. As we recite these passages, we are reminded to atone for sins of arrogance and the intellect. The *zichronos* passages refresh our memory of the *akeidas Yitzchak* (the sacrificing of Yitzchak). *Shofaros*, the Talmud implies, is the means by which the *akeidah* is remembered, as it recalls the horns of the ram sacrificed in place of Yitzchak. The two groups of passages signifying the *akeidah* represent its joint aspects: Yitzchak's willingness to sacrifice his body on the *mizbe'ach*, and Avraham's subordinating his love for his son to Hashem's will, in order to perform the sacrifice. *Zichronos* may represent the total dedication of the body to Hashem, thus atoning for sins of the body. *Shofaros*, on the other hand, may represent the harnessing of our emotions to Hashem, thereby rectifying sins of emotion.

Now we can understand why in the *selichos* we petition

---

4   See *Ohr Yahel* (vol. 2, p. 162) and *Tiferes Yisrael* (*Avos* 4:21 [28]).
5   See Y. S. Hurwitz, *Self Beyond Self* (Feldheim), p. 8.

Hashem's compassion twice in the merit of the *akeidah*: "May He who answered our father Avraham at Mount Moriah, answer us. May He who answered Yitzchak his son when he was bound on the *mizbe'ach*, answer us." What is the difference between the two requests? And how was Avraham's sacrifice at Moriah any different than that of Yitzchak's? But, as we have explained, there were two dimensions to the *akeidah*: the physical sacrifice of Yitzchak as well as the emotional sacrifice of Avraham. Perhaps the first request is made in the merit of Avraham's overcoming his natural love for his son at the *akeidah*, whereas the second request is made in the merit of Yitzchak's willingness to sacrifice his physical being.

We can now return to our original question: Why do we recall the crying of the wicked mother of Sisera to deduce the details of blowing the shofar? Because the shofar reminds us how our forefather Avraham overcame the intense love of a parent for child to offer his son Yitzchak on the *mizbe'ach*. Intense love, longing, and the concern for one's child's welfare are the same emotions that Sisera's mother felt while awaiting the return of her son from the battlefield. Such emotion is felt by all parents.

It is in the merit of Avraham's success at control of instinctive love that we hope to atone for our sins.

Capture the Moment

The symbolic foods on Rosh Hashanah
help create the proper mind-set for the day

The Talmud (*Horayos* 12a) recommends that on Rosh Hashanah a person should eat foods symbolizing a good year. Among these, for example, is the squash, known as *kara*, to symbolize that any evil decrees should be "torn" (*ye-kar-u*); black-eyed peas, or *rubya*, which suggest that our merits be "increased" (*yir-bu*); and dates, or *temarim*, which suggest that our enemies be "destroyed" (*yi-tam-u*).

The Rema (*Orach Chaim* 583:1) also cites the custom of eating apples and honey to symbolize a sweet year. The Mishnah Berurah (*Orach Chaim* 583:5) similarly cites the custom to avoid eating sour foods on Rosh Hashanah, so as not to suggest a less-than-sweet year. Another custom cited by the Rema is to avoid eating nuts, since the numerical value of *egoz*, the Hebrew word for "nut," is equal to that of *chet*, the word for "sin," and we do not want our sins to be recalled on Rosh Hashanah. These customs, though well-known and even enjoyable, may seem rather superficial unless they are understood properly. Clearly, eating a few foods with names that lend themselves to wordplay and suggest a symbolic meaning does not guarantee a positive outcome for the year. What is it, then, that we hope to accomplish?

Rav Shlomo Wolbe (*Alei Shur*, vol. 1, p. 44) offers a fascinating insight into the meaning of Rosh Hashanah. He bases it on a comment in the Jerusalem Talmud regarding Yishmael, Hagar's son. In the reading for the first day of Rosh Hashanah, the Torah relates that after Hagar, Avraham's concubine, was sent away by Avraham with her son, Yishmael took ill. His mother despaired of his life. An angel appeared to Hagar and consoled her, saying that her son would recover, because Hashem had heard his cries *"ba'asher hu sham"* — "in his [Yishmael's] present state" (*Bereishis* 21:17).

The Talmud (*Rosh Hashanah* 16b) understands "in his present state" to mean Yishmael's present conduct. Hashem was not holding Yishmael accountable for his future actions or for the future actions of his descendents, but rather only judging him for his behavior at the time of his illness. Yishmael was thus deserving of having his life spared.

Rabbeinu Chananel (*Rosh Hashanah* 16b) cites yet another comment from the Jerusalem Talmud: Not only was Yishmael not judged with regard to his behavior-to-come, he was not even judged for his past behavior. Thus, Hashem's judgment covers present conduct. If a person atones for past misbehavior, he is guaranteed a favorable judgment.

This, Rav Wolbe explains, is the meaning of judgment on Rosh Hashanah. On this day, every person's actions, speech, and thoughts are examined carefully and judged accordingly. The month of Elul, prior to Rosh Hashanah, affords us an opportunity to clean the stains of past misdeeds by doing *teshuvah*, so that at the moment of judgment we are not found lacking. As long as we capture that moment properly on Rosh Hashanah, we will be judged favorably, regardless of past or future behavior.

Rav Wolbe's explanation lets us appreciate a seeming puzzle. Although Rosh Hashanah marks the first day of the *aseres yemei teshuvah*, the ten days of preparation for Yom Kippur, no *vidui* ("confession") or mention of sin is made during the service. Why is it that we do not express regret for our sins on the very Day of Judgment itself? Because if a person is judged according to his moral status on Rosh Hashanah, the day that marks Hashem's creation of the world, it is important that his thoughts center on Hashem's kingship and not on his own personal status. Thoughts of sin detract from a positive focus and may adversely affect the judgment.

We can now better appreciate the need to eat symbolic foods on Rosh Hashanah. It is not that the foods assist us. Rather, when we reflect on the symbolism of the foods, such as the sweetness of the honey or the significance of the fish head, we create a positive image in our minds, and we begin to reflect a more positive image ourselves, resulting in a more favorable judgment.

Shofar, Shabbos, and Me

The shofar is not blown on Shabbos to acknowledge the message of Shabbos: recognizing one's true self

The Talmud (*Rosh Hashanah* 29b) says that when Rosh Hashanah falls on Shabbos, the shofar is not blown. This prohibition derives from the concern that a person might forget it was Shabbos and carry the shofar in a public domain, thereby transgressing one of the prohibitions of Shabbos.

We must understand why the Rabbis would prohibit the mitzvah of shofar, which is intended to arouse us to *teshuvah* and self improvement, just because a person might forget it was Shabbos. Furthermore, if there is cause for concern, why would they not prohibit blowing the shofar on Rosh Hashanah Shabbos for the same reason that they prohibited the playing of all musical instruments on Shabbos — out of concern that if the instrument breaks, one may try to repair it?

We must first understand the reason for blowing the shofar. The Sefas Emes draws an interesting parallel between the mitzvah of blowing shofar and the creation of man, when Hashem blew life into Adam's nostrils. Let us examine this idea.

Rosh Hashanah marks the anniversary of Creation. The Talmud explains that, in reality, Creation began on the twenty-fifth day of Elul. Six days later, on Rosh Hashanah, Hashem created Adam. Because the human being is the pinnacle of Creation, Rosh Hashanah is considered the birthday of the world, in the same way that a couple celebrate the anniversary of their wedding and not their first date, for the wedding is the goal of the relationship.

The creation of Adam is described as being quite different from the creation of animals. Whereas animal life came into being through the words of Hashem, "Let the earth bring forth living creatures," Adam came to life only when Hashem breathed into his nostrils.

The *Zohar* explains, "When one blows, he draws from his essential nature and expels it into the receiving object." Thus, in blowing into Adam's nostrils to give him life, Hashem instilled a measure of His divinity into the very essence of Adam.[6] This divine spark separates human life from animal life.

Blowing the shofar on Rosh Hashanah commemorates the original breath received on this day. It serves as an eternal reminder for each person to remember his divine essence and to behave accordingly.

This perception of humankind stands in sharp contrast to the media-influenced view we have of ourselves. We are bombarded daily with a media barrage of advertisements and messages that would have us see ourselves as hedonistic animals — following the latest trend, fad, or style. People are actually led to believe

---

6   See *Nefesh Hachaim* (1:15).

that their essence is that of a somewhat sophisticated animal.

Listen to the average child when he or she is asked about the future: "What would you like to be when you grow up?" Likely, the answer will be "a fireman," "a teacher," "a doctor," "a nurse," or some similar occupation. Note, the question was not "What would you like to do when you get older?" or "How would you like to make your money?" but, rather, "What would you like to be?" Young children begin identifying themselves, their being, by profession, because this is how society identifies them.

On Rosh Hashanah, the shofar reminds the Jew that he is a divine being from whom a higher standard of behavior is expected. The Jew is not merely an animal driven by physical pleasure. Nor should he be a creature driven by the desire for high-status jobs, lucrative pay, and various forms of self-aggrandizement.

Let us now try to understand the meaning behind the prohibition of carrying outside on Shabbos. The commentators note that many of the prohibited activities on Shabbos involve creativity. The Torah wants us to cease creating on Shabbos, so that we can recognize Hashem's absolute mastery over the world. Yet this interpretation does not explain the prohibition of carrying outside on Shabbos, since carrying involves no creativity. Why is carrying outside prohibited on Shabbos?

I once heard an explanation for the prohibition of carrying from Rav Michel Twerski of Milwaukee that ties in beautifully with our understanding of the shofar's message on Rosh Hashanah. When making a purchase in a store by check or credit card, or when applying for a job, people are often asked for identification. This usually means the person's license number, social security number, credit card, etc. People are also often identified through their social circle and social status, as revealed by their clothing, the type of car that they drive, or the neighborhood in which they live. One's inner nature is inconsequential insofar as society is concerned. The world at large is much more concerned with a person's monetary worth or social stature than with his character.

Rav Twerski explained that Shabbos is meant for the Jew to reflect on the real meaning of his identity. On Shabbos we desist from those weekday activities that hinder introspection. But we are so influenced by society that we have forgotten how to identify ourselves. Our first thought is to pull out a driver's license, a credit card, the keys to the car, or the keys to the house. After all, that is how society sees us. On Shabbos, however, our pockets are empty. No wallet, no keys.

On Shabbos we are forced to look a little deeper for identification. We come to recognize that the real essence of a person lies in the divine spark within. Thus, Shabbos and shofar provide a similar opportunity: to focus on our true nature and to elevate our standards accordingly.

With Rav Twerski's interpretation we can now understand why the shofar is not blown when Rosh Hashanah falls on Shabbos. It is not necessary to sound the shofar. By observing the laws of Shabbos every week of the year and not carrying outside, the lesson of the shofar is absorbed just as well. In fact, were we to blow the shofar on Shabbos Rosh Hashanah, and come to carry the shofar, the internalized message of Shabbos would be lost for the entire year. That, the Rabbis felt, was too great a price to pay for the message of the shofar on Rosh Hashanah.

We can also understand why the Rabbis did not prohibit sounding the shofar on Shabbos Rosh Hashanah for the same reason that it is prohibited to play all musical instruments on

Shabbos, because of the concern that were it to break one might come to fix it. That would not have been a sufficient reason for excluding the important message of the shofar on Rosh Hashanah. Carrying on Shabbos, however, could undermine the message of the shofar for the remainder of the year.

Rav Shlomo Wolbe sees the idea of personal identification in the Talmud's description of the judgment on Rosh Hashanah. "On Rosh Hashanah, every person passes before Hashem in judgment, just like the B'nei Maron" (*Rosh Hashanah* 18a). The Talmud explains that B'nei Maron is a very narrow overpass through which only one person can pass at a time. What exactly is the significance of B'nei Maron?

Rav Wolbe says that people tend to identify themselves through recognized social labels. We follow the latest trends, fads, and fashions, so that we will be accepted by those around us. We do things in imitation of others, not because we necessarily want or need to do them. Our identity and mission become lost in the drive to conform to social expectation. On Rosh Hashanah each person is judged according to the degree to which his individual potential has been fulfilled. How will the individual answer Hashem's question, "Who are you and what are your goals?" How absurd it would be to answer, "What do you mean? I'm one of the *chevrah* (group)! My goals are like those of everyone else!"

On Rosh Hashanah each person passes before Hashem to be judged, just as at B'nei Maron, individually. Each person stands alone. There is no *chevrah*, no place to lose one's identity and mission. Each person must look within, connect with the divine spark within, and recognize his true purpose in life.

The judgment of Rosh Hashanah, the message of the shofar,

and the meaning of not carrying on Shabbos all have the same function: to remind each of us that we must be more closely linked with our inner selves, and to strive towards realizing our potential. Through this awareness, we can be confident that the new year will be a productive and meaningful one.

The Joyous Awe of Rosh Hashanah

The joy of Rosh Hashanah is the awesome recognition of one's responsibility

Rosh Hashanah is a series of paradoxes. In some ways it is a joyous day: festive meals are served, and we extend joyous greetings to one another. Sin is not even mentioned during the Rosh Hashanah prayers, so as not to detract from our positive focus and cloud the joy of the day.

Yet much of Rosh Hashanah focuses on the fear of judgment. The Hallel, which is usually recited on holidays, is omitted on Rosh Hashanah. As the Talmud puts it, "the Book of Life and Death is opened before Him, and the Jewish people want to sing praises?" (*Rosh Hashanah* 32b). Again, every other Yom Tov we begin the day meal before noon, in order to prevent people from engaging in behavior that resembles fasting. But on Rosh Hashanah, the Mateh Ephraim (597:2) permits eating later, since people are praying for their lives and eating is less important. Apparently, the joy of Yom Tov is subsumed by a fear of judgment. How do the seemingly contradictory emotions of joy and fear coexist on this holiday?

Before answering this paradox, we must examine a more general question. What is the reason for the joy at Jewish life-cycle events? For example, a baby boy is born, and eight days later he is circumcised. Everyone attending the *simchah* experiences great joy and enjoys a beautiful repast. Doesn't it seem rather cruel that the celebrants rejoice while the baby suffers great pain?

Now consider the boy celebrating his bar mitzvah. His father makes a *berachah*, "*Baruch sheptarani me'ansho shelazeh*" — "Blessed is He who has relieved me from this one's liabilities."

The parents seem to be washing their hands of responsibility, yet everyone joyously wishes them "Mazal tov!" It seems so cold. How can people rejoice when this young child is suddenly on his own?

Years later, a young couple stands under the *chuppah*. Having known each other for a relatively short time, they make a commitment to each other for life, sacrificing the freedoms of single life. It ought to be so daunting, yet everyone rejoices! What is the meaning behind the joy?

The common denominator of the above occasions is the acceptance of responsibility. At each of these events individuals stand at a threshold: a door that opens to a more complex and a richer personal identity.

The circumcision marks a Jewish boy's first step in taking on the yoke of responsibility inherent in the sanctity of being a Jew. The bar mitzvah boy accepts personal responsibility for performing mitzvos. He has reached a new stage in life, one that offers more possibilities, deeper satisfactions, greater obligations, and, also, potential pitfalls. At the *chuppah*, a couple accept responsibility for their new status, for the new entity they have become, and for the new family they hope to raise. Jews celebrate accepting responsibility.

Man was not created merely to maintain himself; he was created for a higher purpose. Only when he feels that he is working towards a higher goal can he achieve inner satisfaction. True joy comes from feeling and recognizing the responsibilities each person has been called upon to take on for Hashem. Life-cycle events are accompanied by the rejoicing that comes from moving towards a higher goal.

We can now explain the paradox of Rosh Hashanah. On Rosh Hashanah we are judged for all of our actions. Every good deed is counted and marked for reward; every shortcoming is recorded for retribution. We are reminded that each of us is responsible for our actions. We may be fearful of the possible outcome of the judgment, as we should be if we take it seriously. However, by the same token, the acceptance of this responsibility brings great joy. We realize that there is meaning to our lives, and this knowledge is a source of joy. We must constantly strive towards higher goals. The joy of Rosh Hashanah lies in the recognition of man's potential and the hope that it can yet be fulfilled.

Yom Kippur

The Happiest Day of the Year

Understanding the severity of sin allows us to appreciate the joy of forgiveness

The Talmud (*Ta'anis* 26b) tells us that Yom Kippur and the fifteenth day of Av were the two happiest days of the year. They were so joyous, in fact, that in the times of the Beis Hamikdash (the Holy Temple) the people would hold celebrations to enable eligible young men and women to meet with an eye to marriage. This may seem somewhat strange to us, as few people today would consider Yom Kippur an appropriate time for such events or one of the happiest days in the Jewish calendar. What was the source of this great joy, and why do most of us not experience it today?

A parable may explain our changed perception of Yom Kippur. Two individuals were visiting a doctor's office with similar flu-like symptoms. The physician informs Patient A that he has likely contracted a terrible, life-threatening disease. A few more tests will be necessary to make a precise determination, but Patient A should brace himself for bad news. After the lab results are in, however, the doctor tells the patient that the tests were all negative. He has nothing more serious than a mild flu. After a few days rest, he should be back to his normal self.

We can well imagine Patient A walking out of the doctor's office. Although he appears ill, he nonetheless presents a picture of pure joy. He stops and smiles at everybody, and sniffs the fresh air appreciatively. He has just been granted a new lease on life! The flu symptoms seem hardly to matter now.

Now consider Patient B. The physician tells him right off the bat that he has the flu. He should be back to his normal self after a few days of rest. Patient B leaves the doctor's office grumbling about the physician's inability to relieve his discomfort. How will he endure his aches and pains for another day?!

Although both patients have similar symptoms, one leaves the doctor's office joyously, while the other complains. What has created this difference? Patient A has endured the extremity of fear and has been relieved to learn that everything will be okay. The threat has been lifted. He has received a stay of execution! Patient B, on the other hand, never had reason to think his condition was serious. He wanted to be treated so that his discomfort would be alleviated, but he has not been given anything. Accordingly, he cannot feel joy of relief. In fact, he is rather annoyed by his suffering.

The Talmud calls Yom Kippur one of the happiest days because were we to appreciate the terrible consequences of transgressing Hashem's mitzvos, the joy of being forgiven would be immeasurable. Obviously the day on which the burden of sin was lifted and the fear of punishment removed would be one of the happiest of the year. In the times of the Yom Kippur service in the Beis Hamikdash, the people felt assured of their atonement and thus celebrated accordingly.

Unfortunately, most of us today do not appreciate the gravity of transgressing Hashem's mitzvos. As such, we do not share the same joy of forgiveness on Yom Kippur as described in the Talmud. One who does not feel the danger can hardly experience the relief.

Our lack of appreciating the severity of sin has other ramifications, too. People often have difficulty grasping the concept of rabbinic "fences." There are many acts that were not prohibited by the Torah that still may not be performed. The Rabbis constructed fences that created boundaries far wider than the Torah-stipulated transgressions required. These would prevent people from mistakenly stumbling and trespassing on prohibited soil. The three following examples are suggestive.

Kashrus

The Torah only prohibits the eating of milk and meat that were cooked together. Eating a cold steak and cheese sandwich would be permissible by Torah law, if not for the intercession of rabbinic law. Since the Rabbis were concerned that a person who ate cold dairy and meat might eventually come to eat dairy and meat that had been cooked together, they proscribed the combination altogether. They created yet another fence by requiring a waiting period of some hours between the consumption of a meat meal and the eating of dairy products. Even then, dairy items may not be served on plates used for meat. Moreover, bread that is served at a meat meal may not be eaten later with dairy foods. There are a host of other, complex specifics regarding the preparation and consumption of food deemed dairy and food deemed meat — so many rules and prohibitions emerging out of the simple concern that a Jew might come to transgress the Torah proscription against eating meat cooked with milk!

Shabbos

The Torah prohibits the act of writing on Shabbos. The Rabbis extended this to the handling of a writing utensil; to forbidding commercial transactions that might lead to writing; and even to handling money, which might lead to purchasing and hence to writing.

Constraints Regarding Relationships between Males and Females

The Torah proscribes certain sexual relationships. The Rabbis created a fence such that not only were actual physical intimacies barred, but even being alone with a member of the opposite gender was prohibited, once a girl reaches the age of three and a boy the age of nine (with some exceptions).

Is it ridiculous to carry the concern for sin so far? We have difficulty understanding the reasoning of the Rabbis, as we surely lack their deeper sense of the ramifications of transgression. We must remember that risk is measured when the probability of an occurrence is multiplied by the cost of its occurring. A low probability may seem reassuring; but if the cost of the occurrence is extremely high, we must be especially cautious.

Before the 1980s, tamper-proof packing was virtually nonexistent. But in 1982, seven people in the Chicago area died after taking Tylenol capsules that had been laced with cyanide. These statistically minor events led to a revolution in the technology of product packing. Today, most packaged products come safety-sealed. The cost of these precautionary measures is passed on to the consumer, who is willing to pay for peace of mind — no matter how remote the danger.

The Rabbis' concerns regarding sinful behavior were no different than the concern regarding the cyanide poisoning. They felt it well worth the inconvenience and cost of erecting additional fences, both as barriers to sin and as a testament to the importance of avoiding any encounter with sin. When we do not appreciate the severity of sin, we cannot understand the need for rabbinic fences — and we are unable to appreciate the joy of being absolved of sin.

If we aspire to a joyous Yom Kippur, we must first reflect upon the nature of sin and its consequences and the need to improve our own behavior. Thus, the atonement of Yom Kippur involves effort. Rambam (*Hilchos Teshuvah* 1:3) says that without *teshuvah*, Yom Kippur does not atone for sins. *Teshuvah* itself is a process in which the individual recognizes and takes responsibility for personal sin, regrets the sin, and resolves to improve. Only after we understand the gravity of our actions and undertake to mend our ways can Yom Kippur provide atonement. Then we can merit the gift of Yom Kippur and appreciate the day as one of our happiest, too.

Holy, Holy, Holy

Yom Kippur allows us a glimpse of how to use our body's activities for the service of Hashem

Yom Kippur is often referred to as the *yom hakadosh*, the holy day. Holiness is found in three dimensions of Jewish thought:
- *olam* (literally, world), or space
- *shanah* (literally, year), or time
- *nefesh* (literally, soul), or man

The Beis Hamikdash that stood in Jerusalem — and especially the *kodesh kodashim* (the Holy of Holies section of the Temple) — represented holiness in space. Yom Kippur expresses holiness in time. The *kohen gadol* represented holiness in man.

On Yom Kippur, all three forms of holiness met when the *kohen gadol* entered the *kodesh kodashim*: the holiest man, in the holiest place, on the holiest day. With so much emphasis on holiness, we should try to understand what holiness is. If we do not understand what holiness is, we can hardly be expected to strive for it.

The Torah orders us, "*Kedoshim tihyu ki kadosh Ani*" — "You shall be holy, because I am holy" (*Vayikra* 19:2). The Jewish people are referred to as *goy kadosh*, a holy nation (*Shemos* 19:6). In a literal sense, holiness implies abstinence and separation from the physical world.[1] Man emulates Hashem by separating himself from the physical world, because Hashem — with no physical being or physical needs — is totally without physicality.

However, the Torah never intended for man to divorce himself from his physical drives. In fact, the Torah encourages man to recognize and satisfy his physical desires. The male-female union is considered a mitzvah within the realm of marriage, as is the enjoyment of delicacies on Shabbos, Yom Tov, and at *simchah* occasions.

However, man was charged with maintaining the proper discipline and control over his physical and emotional desires. These are to be directed in the service of Hashem, thereby elevating the physical body to a spiritual level. Thus, the drinking of wine (an intoxicating beverage) that ushers in the Shabbos is called "Kiddush," or "sanctification." Likewise, marriage is called "*kiddushin*" because in marriage man's physical nature is elevated and sanctified.

The *kohen gadol* best personifies the "holy man": his physical nature is employed primarily in the service of Hashem. He is severely restricted in his marital choice — he may marry only a previously unmarried woman from select families. He may not even marry a widow. The *kohen gadol* is also not allowed to enter a cemetery or attend a funeral, even that of a close family member.

However, there was only one *kohen gadol*. Other people were not expected to live with such restrictions. Likewise, Yom Kippur is the day that exemplifies holiness: on Yom Kippur we are separated from all forms of physical pleasure, such as eating, bathing, and marital relations. Yet Yom Kippur is only one day a year;

---

1   See *Mesillas Yesharim*, ch. 13.

no other day is governed by the prohibitions of Yom Kippur.

But if Yom Kippur and the *kohen gadol* were not meant to teach routine conduct, they were meant to be guideposts. From them man can learn that physical pleasure is not an end in itself, but rather it is a vehicle. Every organ of the body must be used appropriately, in the service of Hashem.

In the Shabbos morning prayers, in *Nishmas*, we say:

> Were our mouths as full of song as the sea, and our tongues as full of joyous song as its multitudes of waves, and our lips as full of praise as the breadth of the heavens, and our eyes as bright as the sun and the moon, and our hands as outspread as eagles of the sky, and our feet as swift as hinds — we still could not thank you sufficiently.... The organs that You set within us, and the spirit and soul that You breathed into our nostrils, and the tongues that You placed in our mouths — all of them thank and bless, praise and glorify, exalt and revere, sanctify.... Every mouth shall offer thanks to You; every tongue shall vow allegiance to You; every knee shall bend to You; every spine shall prostrate itself before You; all hearts shall fear You...as it is written: "All my bones shall say, 'Hashem, who is like You?' "

It is only through the complete sanctification of the body that we can see our potential to be *tzelem Elokim*, in the "image of God" — the potential with which we were created.

Rav Shlomo Wolbe (*Alei Shur*, vol. 1, p. 211) explains that this is why the Yom Kippur *vidui* focuses on the sins of the bodily organs. We confess for the sins of hardening of the heart; uttering of the lips; thinking of improper thoughts in one's heart; confessing insincerely with the mouth; bribing of the palms; slandering of the tongue; arrogant tilting of the throat; lustful gazing of the eyes; demonstrating brazenness of the forehead; miserliness of the eyes; stiff-neckedness; running of the feet to do evil; and dealing of the hands in shady business transactions. The sin of not using the organs of the body as Hashem intended is, in some ways, worse than the actual sins themselves.

Imagine the following scenario. Mr. A gives Mr. B a beautiful set of tools as a gift. Mr. B's joyous reaction fills Mr. A with pleasure. A few days later, however, Mr. B becomes angry with Mr. A. Now Mr. B takes his new hammer and proceeds to beat Mr. A with it. Mr. A is injured by the blow, but he is even more distraught because of Mr. B's ingratitude and insensitivity. He has used tools that could build beautiful objects, and debased them through his violent and assaultive behavior to his benefactor. He has perverted their function. In a similar manner, one who sins has taken the body given to him by Hashem for great purposes, and used it to transgress Hashem's will.

Accordingly, if man's source of sin lies in the misuse of his body, that is where *teshuvah* must begin, too. On Yom Kippur we take ourselves to the extremity of physical denial: we abstain from all forms of physical pleasure. We do not eat, drink, bathe, or engage in marital relations.

Again, this is not meant to be normal procedure. But here we follow a principle mentioned by the Rambam: When a person strays to one extreme, the first part of *teshuvah* is to move — temporarily — to the other extreme (*Hilchos Dei'os* 2:2). Since the body has been used for its own gratification rather than in the service of Hashem, it must now be denied that gratification.

Yom Kippur is called the Holy Day, because it gives us an opportunity to glimpse our full potential as a holy people.

Yom Kippur and the Yetzer Hara

The primary challenges of immorality and idolatry play a prominent role in the Yom Kippur service

The Torah reading for a Yom Tov usually reflects or expresses some theme of the Yom Tov. For some Yomim Tovim the connection is quite clear, as on Pesach, when we read about the Exodus from Egypt, and on Shavuos, when we read about the giving of the Torah at Mount Sinai. The connection on other Yomim Tovim, however, is not as clear.

On Rosh Hashanah we read about the birth of Yitzchak. Although there is no obvious connection between Yitzchak and Rosh Hashanah, the Midrash teaches that Avraham and Sarah were "remembered" by Hashem on Rosh Hashanah to bear children. We also read about the *akeidas Yitzchak* on the second day of Rosh Hashanah to recall this great merit on the Day of Judgment.

On Yom Kippur afternoon we read the Torah section of the *arayos*, the prohibited marital relationships (*Vayikra* 18). This seems quite odd, as it has no apparent connection to Yom Kippur. Why was this section chosen?

Rashi (*Megillah* 31a) explains that this section reminds sinners that they should desist from sin, and especially from the sexual offenses which entice a man and for which the inclination is quite strong. Tosafos (ibid.) adds that women commonly adorn themselves in honor of Yom Kippur, and it is therefore necessary to remind people not to stumble in areas of immorality. Rashash (ibid.) sees an allusion in Rashi and Tosafos to the custom mentioned in the Talmud (*Ta'anis* 26b) that on Yom Kippur afternoon, the eligible young women of Jerusalem would dance in the vineyards and try to attract the eyes of eligible young men for the purposes of marriage.[2] It was thus quite timely to read about morality and prohibited marriages on Yom Kippur afternoon.

Tosafos also cites a midrash that explains the Torah reading metaphorically. Just as Hashem has ordered us not to uncover the nakedness of sin, so we beseech Him not to uncover our disgrace in sin, either.

Perhaps we can suggest still another connection. During the times of the Beis Hamikdash an important part of the Yom Kippur service involved the *se'ir shel Azazel*, a goat bearing the sins of the Jewish people. This animal was taken to the wilderness and pushed off a cliff, thereby atoning for the nation's sins. The commentators are perplexed at this near pagan ceremony and try to offer explanations for it.

Ramban and Ibn Ezra understand the procedure of the *se'ir* as something akin to idolatry, fooling the *satan* and preventing him from prosecuting the Jewish people. (This concept is quite complex, and Ramban and Ibn Ezra discuss it in veiled terms. The re-

---

2 See article by Rabbi J. Soloveichik in *Jewish Action* (fall 1987).

sult, however, is that the *se'ir* silences the prosecution for idolatry.) *Hakesav Vehakabalah* similarly suggests that the *se'ir* was meant to mock the ways of the idolators. The animal that was supposed to bear their sins was killed in a cruel and unusual manner and contaminated everyone involved in its preparation. The ceremony was meant to dissuade the Jews from engaging in idolatry. We thus see that an important part of the Yom Kippur service was meant to remove the ugly blot of idolatry from the Jewish people.

The Midrash (*Shir Hashirim* 7:14) says that Hashem created two major lusts in the world: the lust for idolatry and the lust for immorality. The lust for idolatry was removed, but the lust for immorality still remains. Hashem says that whoever can control his desire for immorality will be considered as if he had conquered both desires.

The *se'ir shel Azazel* was meant to counter the lust for idolatry during the times of that lust. However, during the times of the second Beis Hamikdash, the *anshei keneses hagedolah* successfully petitioned Hashem to remove the lust for idolatry (see *Yoma* 69b). Accordingly, once the Beis Hamikdash was destroyed, the Rabbis never felt it necessary to replace the *se'ir* ceremony with anything else, as the lust for idolatry no longer existed. However, immorality, the other major lust, still remains, posing a challenge equal to that of both forms of lust.

It is, therefore, logical that part of the Yom Kippur service should address the remaining lust and aim to diffuse it. Chazal (the Sages) therefore designated the section of the *arayos* to be read on Yom Kippur afternoon, to serve as both a warning and a source of encouragement — that they not allow the inclination towards immorality to become a prosecutor for the Jewish people.

Sukkos

The Joy of Life

Sukkos teaches us that the greatest joy is experienced through simplicity

The Talmud (*Sukkah* 11b) cites two reasons for Sukkos. Rabbi Eliezer says it commemorates the clouds of glory that protected the Children of Israel from the elements during their forty-year trek through the desert. Rabbi Akiva says the holiday commemorates the actual huts that the Children of Israel made for themselves in the desert.

Rabbi Eliezer's opinion is easier to understand. Many of the kindnesses and miracles that Hashem showed our forefathers are marked by holidays or other mitzvos. Pesach recalls the kindness Hashem showed the Jewish people during the Exodus from Egypt. Yom Kippur commemorates Hashem's forgiving the nation the sin of the golden calf. It would make sense, then, that Hashem's great kindness in providing the nation with protection should also be marked with a holiday.

Rabbi Akiva's opinion, however, is more difficult to understand. Why should we celebrate as mundane an activity as building a hut? What lasting significance is there in the building of temporary housing during the forty years in the desert, that it should require a holiday commemorating it?

The Tur asks another question: why is Sukkos celebrated in the autumn? Since the holiday marks events that took place in the desert when the Jews left Egypt, it would be logical for it to be celebrated after Pesach — the holiday recalling the Exodus — in the spring, not six months later. The closeness of Sukkos to Yom Kippur also implies some sort of connection between these two holidays.

Finally, in our prayers Sukkos is referred to as *zeman simchaseinu*, our joyous time. Why is the holiday of Sukkos, more than any other holiday, associated with joy?

In the human experience, pursuit of joy and happiness is one of the most natural and important drives. People spend much of their lives seeking bigger and better diversions and amusements in their search for happiness. Yet, strangely, the more a person concentrates on happiness, the more the goal seems to evade him. Yesterday's model luxury car, dream home, or entertainment is rendered meaningless as we run after today's newer and fancier model. The Rabbis' dictum (*Koheles Rabbah* 1:34) is so true: "He who has one hundred wants two hundred, and he who has two hundred wants four hundred." A person cannot achieve the elusive goal of satisfaction, for the vicious cycle caused by his insatiable desire for bigger and better is never-ending.

The sukkah signals an end to this cycle; it marks a retreat to simplicity. The rickety walls and open roof of the temporary structure remind us of the transiency of life. We recognize how precious it is. Life is too valuable to squander on an endless pursuit of material comforts. Suddenly we realize that happiness was sought in the wrong places. The sukkah allows us to face the beauty of nature at close range — the sunset, the outdoors, and the harvest. What we need is to be found right outside our front door. True joy lies in the simplicity of the sukkah, more so than in the luxury of the house.

The Midrash offers a fascinating insight into appreciating life. After the sixth day of Creation the Torah says, "Hashem saw all that He created, and behold, it was very good." The Midrash comments that "very good" refers to death. How does the Midrash arrive at this insight? How can death be considered "very good"?

Consider an existence without death. If man lived forever, his life would be meaningless. Why should he wish to improve his character, to develop relationships, or achieve anything? Man would procrastinate, knowing he had endless time to confront his tasks. Only because man knows that death exists, and that he will not live forever, do goals take on greater urgency. Then time is recognized as a precious commodity. We can appreciate life more because we know it is so limited.

There are many stories told of families in which one member has a terminal illness. The last weeks or months of this person's life are often the most meaningful for the family. Nothing is taken for granted, and things that had not seemed important are now regarded differently. Work at the office, or similar commitments, aren't as important as a simple outing, or just spending time together. The realization of the temporary nature of life can bring with it an unprecedented joy.

Now we can better understand Sukkos. The re-creation of our forefathers' temporary huts shows us how to appreciate and enjoy life by focusing on its transience. That is why Sukkos, more than any other holiday, is called the time of our joy, because it contains within it the secret of happiness.

And what better time to celebrate Sukkos than right after Yom

Kippur, with its focus on judgment? As we reflect on death and the ephemeral nature of life, we appreciate life even more, and we are ready to absorb the lessons of Sukkos and rejoice.

Fulfilling the Will of Hashem

The sukkah provides a model to determine a person's true commitment to Hashem

The Talmud (*Avodah Zarah* 3b) relates how the nations of the world complained to Hashem that they wish to be rewarded like the Jews. Hashem explains that they did not accept His Torah when it was offered to them like the Jews did; thus, they do not deserve the rewards. The nations retort that Hashem had intimidated the Jews into receiving the Torah at Mount Sinai, informing them that a refusal meant they would die. Had they been intimidated like the Jews, they would also have accepted the Torah. Hashem responds that the Jewish people had only been threatened after they had said, *"Na'aseh v'nishma"* ("We will do and we will listen"). Since they had committed themselves, Hashem wanted to make sure they would follow through. Those nations that had expressed skepticism from the very beginning did not deserve further encouragement, and were not deserving of any reward.

Nonetheless, Hashem decides to give the nations a final opportunity to prove their allegiance, and He gives them the mitzvah of sukkah. The nations work diligently to build their sukkos, but Hashem brings out a sweltering hot sun. The nations leave the sukkos, kicking the walls in disgust, showing their lack of commitment to even this one mitzvah.

The Talmud then asks: How does leaving their sukkos show that they lack commitment? Surely a Jew would also leave his sukkah if he was uncomfortable; especially since we are exempt from the sukkah in case of discomfort? The answer is that a Jew would leave, but he would not kick the walls.

The entire account is difficult to understand. First of all, why would Hashem choose the mitzvah of sukkah for the nations rather than some other mitzvah? And, once the mitzvah has been chosen, why would Hashem make it too difficult to keep? Why offer a reward for a task that is too difficult to accomplish? And finally, why is the Jew exempted from sitting in the sukkah when he is uncomfortable — especially since no such exemption exists for any other mitzvah?

We can answer these questions in the following manner:

Rav Shlomo Wolbe says we can learn about a person's commitment to mitzvos by observing his reaction when he is released from performing that mitzvah. A person may fulfill a mitzvah, in all its details, by rote, not necessarily because he feels a commitment to Hashem. Should a situation arise when he is unable to perform the mitzvah, he is only too happy to avoid the expenditure of time and energy. However, if the person is disappointed that he cannot perform the mitzvah, he shows a sincere commitment and interest in doing Hashem's will; he is saddened when he cannot fulfill it.

The Rabbis compared the observance of sukkah to the obser-

Fulfilling the Will of Hashem 71

vance of all the other mitzvos in the Torah (liturgy for Shacharis, second day of Sukkos). The Torah exempts the Jew from sitting in the sukkah when he is uncomfortable in order to examine his attitude towards all the mitzvos. If he feels disappointment at being unable to fulfill Hashem's mitzvah, we recognize he sincerely wants to fulfill Hashem's mitzvos, and he is rewarded accordingly. If, however, he is happy to move back indoors, his initial commitment towards the mitzvah must be weak.

Hashem chose the mitzvah of sukkah to give to the nations for the same reason: to serve as a test case for their attitude towards all the mitzvos. By making the day extremely uncomfortable, Hashem tested the extent of their commitment. When the other nations kicked the sukkah in disgust, they revealed their true intentions. They were not so much interested in serving Hashem as receiving the benefits of the service. The ultimate reward for a mitzvah does not serve as payment for the mere observance of details but rather for a total dedication to Hashem's service.

Let us delve a little deeper.

Hashem manifests His desire for man's service through the mitzvos. Yet the mitzvah must never be confused as an end in itself, but should be seen as a means of moving toward the goal of serving Hashem. Once this lesson has been absorbed, one's attitude toward a lost mitzvah will be radically changed. If the reason for performing the mitzvah is to fulfill Hashem's will, then an inability to perform the mitzvah is also Hashem's will. The same Commander who willed the mitzvah fulfilled under certain circumstances also willed that it not be done under other circumstances.

Rabbi Zev Leff relates an incident that occurred in his synagogue in Miami Beach. An elderly woman informed him that her husband's doctor had forbidden him to fast on Yom Kippur, but her husband was not planning on heeding the doctor's orders. She asked Rabbi Leff to convince her husband not to endanger his health. Rabbi Leff confirmed the woman's account with the physician and then spoke to the man. In his situation there was no mitzvah whatsoever to fast. In fact, the Torah requires a dangerously ill person to eat on Yom Kippur. The elderly man was adamant, and said, "Rabbi, I am probably over twice your age. Never have I eaten on Yom Kippur, and nothing you say will stop me from fasting on Yom Kippur!"

Rabbi Leff was taken aback, but said, "You are right. I cannot force you to eat on Yom Kippur. But if I hear that you fasted on Yom Kippur, you will never get another *aliyah* to the Torah in this shul again!"

Now it was the elderly man's turn to be surprised. "What does getting an *aliyah* have to do with anything?"

The rabbi retorted, "You are an idolator, and an idolator cannot get an *aliyah*!"

The gentleman was visibly upset. "How dare you call me an idolator! I am an observant Jew!"

Rabbi Leff explained, "I have told you that Hashem requires you to eat on Yom Kippur, but you feel that Yom Kippur is more important than your health. Idolatry means putting the will of other authorities before the will of Hashem. It makes no difference if that authority is called Ba'al, Zeus, or Yom Kippur! It is all idolatry!"

When a Jew finds it too uncomfortable to sit in the sukkah, he may be disappointed that Hashem does not want his observance of this mitzvah, but he accepts it as the will of Hashem. He realizes that he will have to fulfill the will of Hashem some other way.

He hopes that next time he will be deserving of having his service accepted.

The other nations, though, do not share this outlook. From their viewpoint the mitzvah is a goal, not merely a means. When they are unable to sit in the sukkah, they are angry at Hashem. They exclaim, "How can You first tell me to build a sukkah, and then make it unbearable to sit there?" Their attitude shows that they are not truly interested in serving Hashem, but rather in performing the details of the mitzvah and then claiming the reward. But Hashem's reward is reserved only for those who are sincerely motivated to serve Him in the way that He sees fit, and not the way they see fit.

Circles of Significance

There are four characteristics of the circle that make circle-dancing an important part of Sukkos

The Tosafos Yom Tov (*Rosh Hashanah* 1:2) points out that the Talmud makes an interesting distinction between Sukkos and the other holidays. Whereas the other holidays are referred to as *chag hamatzos* (the holiday of matzos), and *chag hashavuos* (the holiday of Shavuos), Sukkos is referred to merely as *chag* (the holiday). He explains that the word *"chag"* comes from *"chug,"* a circle. This alludes to the circle of dancing that takes place during the Sukkos festivities at the Simchas Beis Hasho'eivah. Because dancing plays such a central role in celebrating the holiday, it is identified as the "dancing holiday." Yet we must still understand why the dancing, and especially circle-dancing, is so connected to Sukkos. We offer a few explanations:

1. A major theme of Sukkos is the unity of the Jewish community. The sukkah unifies all Jews within its walls. To illustrate this

unity, the Midrash draws a parallel between Jews and the four species of plants that are waved during Sukkos. The *esrog* (citron) has a beautiful fragrance and a pleasant taste. This represents vividly the Jew who has both Torah knowledge and does good deeds. The *lulav* (date palm) bears delicious fruit but, without fragrance, represents the Jew with Torah knowledge who is not yet characterized by good deeds. The *hadassim* (myrtle branches) have a pleasant fragrance but no taste and represent the Jew who performs good deeds, but does not accompany them with Torah scholarship. Finally, the simple *aravah* (willow branch) has neither taste nor fragrance, and represents the Jew lacking in good deeds and Torah scholarship. In the service of Hashem, these species are held together while we perform the mitzvah of the Four Species. If one is missing, the mitzvah cannot be performed. Similarly, all Jews must join in the service of Hashem — each plays an important role. The absence of even one Jew prevents every other Jew from fulfilling the will of Hashem properly.

The circle-dancing alludes to this unity, for each point on a circle's rim is equidistant from the center.[1] Likewise, each Jew is important in regard to the larger community. It makes no difference how great or lowly he may be, each and every Jew has an important role to fulfill, and he is equally connected to the "nerve-center" of the Jewish people.

2. Again, a circle has no beginning or end; it goes round and round without end. In this endless circle, we see the eternity of

---

1   In a similar vein, Rav Wolbe once explained that the circle-dancing on Shavuos, where participants all join hands in one large circle, is reminiscent of the unity that existed at Mount Sinai before the Jews could receive the Torah (*Shemos* 19:2 and *Rashi*).

the Jewish nation. On Sukkos we leave the safety and security of our beautiful houses and dwell in simple, temporary huts. Without the shelter of a roof, prey to the elements, the Jew is justified in fearing for his safety. What future can there be in a temporary hut measured against a sturdy and comfortable house? Yet the simple Sukkah-Jew survives, year after year, outliving the powerful armies of his enemies throughout the ages.

On Sukkos many animals were sacrificed in the Beis Hamikdash. Fourteen lambs were offered every day, while the number of bulls sacrificed decreased every day. On the first day thirteen bulls were brought, twelve were offered on the second day, eleven on the third day, and so on — a total of seventy bulls during Sukkos. To the Rabbis[2] the seventy powerful bulls symbolized the seventy nations of the world, whose control and influence were decreasing. However, the weak lambs, representing the Children of Israel, would remain unchanged, a stable presence among the stronger and more powerful nations.[3] Again, the lesson of Sukkos is one of encouragement and hope for the Jewish people.

3. The circle also protects what it encompasses.[4] This reminds us

---

2 See *Rashi, Bamidbar* 29:11.

3 I am reminded of Mark Twain's famous comments, "The Egyptian, the Babylonian, and the Persian rose, filled the planet with sound and splendor, then faded to dream-stuff and passed away: the Greek and the Roman followed, and made a vast noise, and they are gone. Other peoples have sprung up and held their torch high for a time, but it burned out, and they sit in twilight now, or have vanished. The Jew saw them all, beat them all, and is now what he always was..." ("Concerning the Jew," *Harper's Magazine*, 1897).

4 This symbolism is also seen in the bride circling her groom under the *chuppah*, thereby protecting him from external temptations (Aryeh

how the Cloud of Glory surrounded the Jewish people in the desert, protecting them from the elements. The sukkah, enclosing its occupants, represents the cloud and serves as a reminder of Hashem's protection. So, too, the circle-dance reminds us of Hashem's protection.

4. The circle-dance has additional relevance for the holiday. In any dance, we lift the legs and bring them down again to the floor. In the circle-dance, these steps are repeated as the circle moves round and round. The steps have meaning beyond the dance.

At the end of Yom Kippur, with its high aspirations and resolutions, the Jew's hopes and efforts for a marked improvement are often dashed at the first sign of difficulty. A minor setback might depress us with the realization that our aspirations were not as realistic as we had hoped. There is a real danger that the hard-won gains of the High Holiday season could be quickly lost.

The Torah, therefore, requires us to rejoice on Sukkos, right after Yom Kippur, to give us a sense of hope and confidence. We dance, lifting our feet high, and then bringing them down, a step forward and a step backward. Even if we fall back one step, we cannot let it stop us. We move forward, one step and then another. That is how the circle of life works, progress may be followed by relapse, but every relapse is followed by progress, one step back — but then another step forward.

Thus the circular dancing of Sukkos speaks to us. The dancing of Simchas Beis Hasho'eivah, the Hoshana circuits, and the Simchas Torah *hakafos* serve as a call to unite the Jewish people, as a reminder of the eternity of the Jewish people, as a reminder of Hashem's protection, and as a source of hope and encouragement to improve ourselves.

Kaplan, *Made in Heaven*, p. 158).

The Atonement of Sukkos

The sin of idolatry is rectified by the sukkah, leading the way to the rebuilding of the Beis Hamikdash

In the *bentching* (Grace after Meals) of Sukkos, it is our custom to add a special *Harachaman* prayer shortly before the end: "*Harachaman Hu yakim lanu es sukkas David hanofales*" — "May the Compassionate One erect for us the fallen booth of David." This is a reference to the destruction of the Beis Hamikdash, which we hope will be rebuilt speedily in our days.

Yet what is the connection between the rebuilding of the Beis Hamikdash and Sukkos, more so than any other holiday?

To answer this question we must first examine the causes for the destruction and how these sins are to be rectified. The Be'er Yosef (vol. 2, p. 302) cites a poignant midrash (*Pesichta d'Eichah Rabasi*) regarding the destruction of the first Beis Hamikdash. At the time of the destruction, each of the patriarchs and matriarchs pleaded with Hashem to have compassion upon the Jewish people, but to no avail. Then Rachel came before Hashem and pleaded, "Master of the Universe! You know how much my husband Yaakov loved me, and how he worked seven years for my hand. My father wanted to trick Yaakov and give him my sister as a wife instead. I was very troubled by this, so I made up a secret sign through which Yaakov would know if he was marrying me or my sister. Later, when the time came for us to wed, I had compassion on my sister and wanted to spare her the shame, so I taught her the secret sign. To shield my sister, I overcame my desire to marry my beloved. If I, a mere mortal, could restrain my jealousy and not have my sister shamed, You, O Great and Compassionate One, should surely restrain your jealousy from the idols and spare the Jewish people from pain."

Immediately Hashem's compassion was aroused, and He said, "Rachel, for your sake I will yet return the Jewish people to their homeland."

The Be'er Yosef asks why Rachel's request should carry any more weight than those of the other patriarchs. Surely the other patriarchs' prayers were no less sincere, nor were they any less righteous than Rachel. He explains that the primary sin that led to the destruction of the first Beis Hamikdash was the rampant idolatry throughout the land. The Talmud (*Yoma* 9b) expounds on a passage in *Yeshayah* (28:20), that when Menashe, the king of Yehudah, erected an idol in the *kodesh kodashim*, Hashem's jealousy was like that of a woman whose husband has just brought a rival wife into the first wife's private chambers. This jealousy led to the destruction of the Beis Hamikdash.

Rachel, the midrash explains,[5] pleaded with Hashem that she had suffered a similar indignity when her sister Leah was given to

---

5 Cited in *Rashi, Yirmiyahu* (31:14).

her husband Yaakov as a wife. Yet Rachel restrained her jealousy out of compassion for her sister, to protect her from public shame. If so, Rachel argued, surely Hashem could restrain His jealousy and show compassion for the Jewish people. This was an argument that Hashem could not refute, and in Rachel's merit the people would be redeemed.

Sukkos atones for the sin of idolatry. The Nesivos Shalom (*Sukkos*, p. 200) sees the sukkah as a *chuppah*, Hashem's inner chambers, into which is brought the Jewish people, His bride. Thus we have great joy on Sukkos, the joy of a wedding between Hashem and His chosen people, as it says in *Shir Hashirim* (1:4), "*Hevi'ani hamelech chadarav nagilah v'nismechah bach*" — "The King has brought me into His inner chambers; we will be glad and rejoice with You."

Sukkos thus becomes the complete commitment of Hashem and the Jewish people to one another; akin to the total commitment, under the *chuppah*, of the bride and groom to each other. This total commitment rules out any rival relationship, thus atoning for the sin of idolatry so prevalent during the time of the first Beis Hamikdash. Each time we *bentch* on Sukkos, then, we pray that in the merit of the commitment of sukkah we should also merit the rebuilding of the lost Beis Hamikdash.

Hoshana Rabbah, Shemini Atzeres, and Simchas Torah

Prayers for Rain

Two days and two types of prayers are needed to provide us with the blessing of rain

The Talmud (*Rosh Hashanah* 15a) says that on Sukkos the world is judged, and the year's rain supply is determined. Yet no prayers for rain are said during Sukkos, as rain would keep us from the sukkah. In fact, the Talmud considers rain during Sukkos a curse, a message from Hashem that He is not interested in the Jewish people's service in their sukkahs. Only on Hoshana Rabbah, the last day of Sukkos, do prayers address our need for water, implying that the decision for rain is reached on the last day of Sukkos.

It seems strange, therefore, that *Tefillas Geshem*, the prayer for rain, is not said until the day after Sukkos, on Shemini Atzeres. What could the prayer for rain accomplish after the decision has already been made and sealed? It would seem more appropriate to say the prayer on Hoshana Rabbah rather than on Shemini Atzeres.

A similar question can be asked about our prayers throughout the year. If man's fate has already been decided on Rosh Hashanah and Yom Kippur, what does it help to pray for specific situations such as illnesses or financial success during the year? How can the decision be changed?

Perhaps we can understand this idea by examining the Torah's account of Creation. On the third day of Creation the Torah says, "The earth sprouted forth vegetation: herbage yielding seed of its own kind and trees yielding fruit, each containing seeds of its own kind" (*Bereishis* 1:12). On the sixth day of Creation, however, it says, "Now all the trees of the field were not yet on the earth and all the herbs of the field had not yet sprouted, because Hashem had not sent rain upon the earth, and there was no man to work the soil" (ibid. 2:5). The passages seem to contradict one another. Did the vegetation sprout forth on the third day of Creation or the sixth day?

Rashi cites the Talmud's interpretation (*Chullin* 60b) that while Hashem created the vegetation on the third day, it did not actually sprout until man was created. Hashem would only allow the vegetation to sprout after man would pray for it. Hashem wanted prayer to be a necessary part of the fulfillment of His will, not so much because He needs it, but rather because man must know where to turn for the fulfillment of his needs.

The Talmud is teaching us a fascinating insight into the mechanics of prayer. The purpose of prayer is not so much to change Hashem's will, as it were, as to bring about Hashem's will. Even after Hashem wills something, He may still not perform until man makes the proper request in his prayers.

We can now understand the purpose of prayer throughout the year. Even if it has been determined on Rosh Hashanah that a person should be successful, it is still necessary to pray for Hashem's will to be actualized.

This concept may also help us understand another difficult

passage. The Talmud (*Yevamos* 64a) says that the matriarchs all had difficulty conceiving because Hashem desires the prayers of the righteous. How are we to understand a compassionate God who holds back a woman's greatest joy in order to hear her heartfelt pleas? But, as explained, Hashem created spiritual laws of nature as He created physical laws of nature. As a person cannot ignore the physical laws of nature in bringing about a desired effect, so the spiritual need for prayer, and especially the prayers of the righteous, cannot be ignored either.

This may be the basis of praying for rain on Shemini Atzeres. The decision regarding rainfall is reached on Hoshana Rabbah, but that does not yet guarantee its fulfillment. Only the following day on Shemini Atzeres, when we are no longer required to sit in the sukkah, do we pray for the actual rain itself.

Victors in Judgment

Two days to mark the victory of the community and of the individual

The *Midrash Tehillim* (17:5) cites an interesting reason for the mitzvah of *lulav* and *esrog*. On Rosh Hashanah all the nations of the world are brought before Hashem in judgment. When the defendants leave the courtroom, however, it is not clear who has prevailed in judgment. When Sukkos arrives, and the Jewish people take up the *lulavim* in their right hands and the *esrogim* in their left, it is as if they are raising high a banner, announcing to the world that they have been victorious. And when on Hoshana Rabbah they take the *aravos* and circle the *mizbe'ach* seven times, the Heavenly angels rejoice and say, "The Children of Israel have been victorious! The Children of Israel have been victorious!"

We should explain how carrying the *lulav* represents the banner of victory in judgment more so than any other mitzvah. Also, a simple question may be asked: If it is already evident on the first day of Sukkos — upon taking the *lulav* — who has been victorious, what more do we learn seven days later on Hoshana Rabbah? What does the *aravah* add that we do not already know from the *lulav*?

Previously[1] we cited the midrash that compares the Four Species to four types of Jews. The *esrog*, with both taste and aroma, is compared to the Jew who has Torah and good deeds. The *lulav*, with taste but no scent, represents the Jew who has Torah but is lacking in good deeds. The myrtle branches have a pleasant aroma but no taste, symbolizing the Jew with good deeds but no Torah knowledge. The *aravah*, or willow, having neither taste or scent, represents the Jew without Torah scholarship or good deeds.

On the first day of Sukkos we take the Four Species together, representing the unity of all Jews, those who are righteous together with those who are less than righteous. By displaying the combined strength of our people, even after they have been judged, we show that the judgment has not had a detrimental effect on the nation as a whole. This is not to say, however, that the individual Jew can avoid judgment. Often a victory in war brings with it many casualties. The *lulav* and *esrog* demonstrate the victory of the nation, yet they say nothing about the status of any individual Jew in receiving judgment.

On Hoshana Rabbah, however, we take the lone *aravah*, representing the Jew lacking Torah and mitzvos, and circle the *mizbe'ach*. The symbolism is clear: after being linked to the more righteous members of the community for the six days, even the simple Jew emerges victorious from judgment. The positive influence of the community has affected the plain Jew. On Hoshana Rabbah the *aravah* reinforces the message conveyed by the *lulav* during Sukkos. Not only the community has been judged favorably; the ordinary Jew, too, can rejoice in his victory.

---

1   See essay "Circles of Significance."

The Simchah and the Torah

Getting the most from the finale of a marathon holiday period

I was recently struck by the stark contrast between the High Holiday season — where one holiday seems to tumble over the heels of another — and the long period of calm that follows. We feel the mounting excitement in the month before Rosh Hashanah, the increase of awe and reflection, maintained through Rosh Hashanah and Yom Kippur, leading into the joy and exuberance of Sukkos, and culminating in the crescendo of Simchas Torah — before finally settling down for the long winter stretch.

Simchas Torah serves as a bridge between the intense spiritual high of the holidays and the relative quiet of the next six or seven month season (depending on whether or not it is a leap year), broken only by Chanukah and Purim. In effect, Simchas Torah serves as a cushion, breaking our fall into a normal routine.

And yet, practically, Simchas Torah does not always seem to provide that cushion. Rather than being revitalized in our commitment to Torah and its study, we often feel in the aftermath of the holiday "all yontifed out." Even worse, it sometimes seems that the joy of the Torah hasn't left any lasting impression at all. How can we lock in the warmth and enthusiasm from the holiday season?

With Simchas Torah we celebrate the completion of the Torah cycle. Logically the celebration can best be appreciated by those who have actually completed the Torah. Much of the preparation for Simchas Torah reflects our year-round relationship with Torah. The returns are commensurate with the investment. The greater one's enthusiasm and interest in Torah study, the greater the joy will be on Simchas Torah.

Witness Simchas Torah at any yeshivah or shul where yeshivah students are present. To paraphrase a statement in the Talmud: "Anyone who hasn't experienced a yeshivah Simchas Torah celebration hasn't seen true joy." It can be seen and heard in the lively chorus of sung-hoarse voices singing the same refrain over and over: *Toras Hashem temimah* (Hashem's Torah is wholesome and invigorating).... *Ashrei ha'am shekachah lo* (Fortunate is the nation who is thus situated).... *Ashrei ish shelo yishkachecha* (Fortunate is the person who does not forget you). It can be seen in the circle of students throwing themselves into the service of Hashem — singing and dancing together, hand-in-hand, drenched in sweat. The pure joy on their faces is indescribable. It is an atmosphere that is both lively and serious.[2]

---

[2] Rav Shlomo Wolbe encouraged the yeshivah students to wear their hats and jackets during the Simchas Torah dancing, saying the Simchas Torah dancing is no less holy than the Yom Kippur davening. He would quote Rav Yerucham, *zt"l*, that he wasn't sure what pleases Hashem more, the Yom Kippur davening or the Simchas Torah dancing (*Kuntres Adam Bikar*, p. 28).

Imagine the joy of a couple at their daughter's wedding. They have nurtured this young woman since birth, concerned themselves with all aspects of growth, sacrificed so much for her, and watched her bloom into the beautiful bride now standing under the *chuppah*. Their faces glow — it is *their simchah*!

The yeshivah students, too, have lovingly nurtured the Torah — as it, too, has nurtured them. They have concerned themselves with its every facet and nuance. They have sacrificed so much for it, and watched it bloom and flourish. Now, as the Torah stands gloriously at the center of the stage in its own holiday, their faces glow — it is *their simchah*. It is the lively joy of celebration, yet it is also the serious joy of spiritual accomplishment. There can be no doubt about the long-lasting effect of their celebration. It will light up the cold, dark, winter months that follow.

But Torah was not meant to remain the private property of the yeshivah student. Its legacy should be shared by each and every Jew. The true joy of Simchas Torah could be felt by any Jew — if he allows himself to sample the richness and beauty of the Torah throughout the rest of the year.

Of course, there are many reasons offered by people who cannot find the time to study. However, hectic work schedules, family responsibilities, and even communal commitments cannot satisfy the Jewish soul's need for spiritual fulfillment. Without an investment in serious Torah study, the impact of Simchas Torah, as the culmination of the High Holiday period, will be minimal.

Toras Hashem temimah meshivas nafesh — Hashem's Torah is wholesome and invigorating for the soul!

Chanukah

Chanukah and the Secret of Beginnings

The danger, victory, and celebration of Chanukah all focus on the importance of creating holy beginnings

The Talmud (*Shabbos* 21b) begins its discussion of the Chanukah holiday by asking *"Mai Chanukah?"* — "What is Chanukah?" It then proceeds to relate the story of the war the Chashmonaim waged against the Syrian-Greek armies, and the miracle of the flask of oil that lasted for eight days.

The question seems to be a bit strange. Earlier the Talmud had discussed various details about the Chanukah candles; surely it was aware of Chanukah. What was so unclear about the holiday that the question was needed: "What is Chanukah?"

Rashi explains that the Talmud was trying to identify which miracle Chazal felt should be commemorated. Not every miracle in Jewish history is marked by a holiday. The Talmud is asking which part of the Chanukah miracle was deserving of an eternal commemoration. Perhaps we can understand this question a little differently, though.

Rav Tzadok HaKohen (*Tzidkas Tzaddik* 119) offers an interesting insight into the nature of names. A name, he explains, is the key that unlocks the essence of the person or thing it represents. It is not merely a means of identification; the name actually defines the very nature. Accordingly, it is necessary to have a clear understanding of the essence in order to name something properly.[1] The Talmud therefore asks, "*Mai Chanukah?*" meaning how does the name "Chanukah" reflect the essence of the holiday?

The Talmud relates how the Chashmonaim regained control of the Beis Hamikdash after defeating the Syrian Greek armies. They wanted to kindle the menorah but could find no pure oil. The Greeks had deliberately contaminated all the oil in the area. One little flask of oil, with the seal of the *kohen gadol*, was finally found. It contained enough oil to fuel the menorah for one day, however a miracle happened and it burned for eight days. The following year the Rabbis declared these days a holiday.

This, too, requires explanation. How does the miracle of the oil reflect the essence of the holiday more than, say, the actual victory of the war? Furthermore, what does it have to do with the name "Chanukah"?

Let us examine the word "*chanukah*," or dedication. It is closely related to the word "*chinuch*," meaning education. How are dedication and education related?

There is an insightful Rashi regarding the incident where Avraham hears that Lot, his nephew, has been captured (*Bereishis* 14:14). The Torah says about Avraham, "*Vayarek es*

---

[1] This is the great wisdom shown by Adam when he named all the animals (*Bamidbar Rabbah* 19:3). He analyzed the nature of each animal and called it by an appropriate name.

chanichav" — "he armed his disciples." Rashi, in explaining the word "*chanichav*," his disciples, understands the word "*chinuch*" to mean entering on a new endeavor, similar to educating a child (*chanoch lana'ar*), the dedication of the *mizbe'ach* (*chanukas hamizbe'ach*), and the dedication of the Beis Hamikdash (*chanukas habayis*). What again is the connection?

Rav Shlomo Wolbe[2] describes a principle he refers to as "*sod hahaschalah*," the secret of the beginning. The Torah places a special importance on beginnings. The reason is simple: the foundation of a project is its most important part. If a building's foundation is solid, it can survive later structural defects and stresses. If, however, the foundation is weak, then any later defects — even minor ones — can be catastrophic.

For this reason, we must be especially careful at the beginning of any project to ensure that it gets off to a flawless start. We find, for example, during the eight days devoted to the dedication of the *mishkan* in the desert, considerable attention was paid to every detail. Special offerings were brought, much of the service was done by Moshe himself, and the *kohanim* could not leave the service for any reason. These strict requirements were necessary only during the dedication, to ensure a solid foundation.

An individual once approached Rav Simcha Wasserman, trying to justify his praying at the local non-Orthodox synagogue. He claimed that while the synagogue may not have been Orthodox, the services themselves were practically identical. Rav Wasserman responded by telling of two trains at the station, on parallel tracks. A passenger boarding one train might not see a

---

2   Heard in a *va'ad* in Yeshivas Be'er Ya'akov, summer 1979. (Cf. *Alei Shur*, vol. 2, p. 341.)

difference, assuming both trains would end at the same place since they were on parallel tracks. The truth is, however, that the tracks only seem to be parallel, since they diverge imperceptibly. Eventually, the tracks end up miles apart. The same is true of the synagogues, Rav Simcha concluded, for right now they may seem to be alike, but they are headed in different directions. Later, the differences will be all too clear.

This, too, Rav Wolbe explains, is why close attention must be paid to the education of children. The essence of *chinuch*, or education, as seen from the root of the word, is a dedication of sorts. It establishes the foundation of the child's pursuits and goals, and as such must be planned as carefully as possible.

The Talmud (*Sukkah* 42b) mentions that when a child first begins to speak, the parents should teach him "*Torah tzivah lanu Moshe*," "Moshe commanded us the Torah." The *Yalkut Shimoni* (*Ekev* 871) says further that if parents do not begin their child's instruction in language by teaching him Torah, it is as if they bury their child. Without a proper start, success in education is doubtful at best.

The *Sefer Rokeach* (ch. 296, cited in *Sefer Hanhagas Chinuch*) describes the ancient custom of introducing a Jewish child to the study of Torah. Eyes covered by the tallis enwrapping him to keep him from seeing anything impure, the young child was brought to his rebbe's home to be taught *alef-beis*. The rebbe would then dab honey on the letters of the *alef-beis* and coax the child to lick them, allowing him to experience the sweet taste of Torah. He says one must be careful not to change any part of this custom, as the child's success in Torah studies is greatly affected by his first experience, which must be totally pure.

Chanukah and the Secret of Beginnings

Tosafos (*Chagigah* 15a) quotes a *Yerushalmi* on the passage in *Koheles* (7:8), "*Tov acharis davar meireishiso*" — "The end of something is better than its beginning." One interpretation sees the success of an endeavor depending mainly on its beginning. The *Yerushalmi* then relates a story about Elisha ben Avuyah, the rabbi from the Tannaic period who strayed from the path of Torah. Avuyah, Elisha's father, had invited many of the Jerusalem scholars to the circumcision of his son. During the celebration, Rabbi Eliezer and Rabbi Yehoshua began discussing Torah with such intensity that a celestial fire surrounded them. When Avuyah saw this fire, he was impressed. He declared he wanted his son Elisha to dedicate his life to the study of Torah so he could merit such honor. The *Yerushalmi* continues that since his father's intentions were not pure, Elisha's Torah could not protect him from foreign influences, and he later became a heretic.

The story is difficult to understand. First, why should Elisha be held accountable for his father's intentions? Also, does the Talmud not teach (*Pesachim* 50b) that, "A person should always engage in Torah study and mitzvos, even for ulterior motives, for eventually his motives will become pure"? If the Talmud encourages study for the wrong reasons, why should Elisha suffer for it?

It is important to note, though, that this story took place at Elisha's circumcision. The bris milah marks the dedication of a Jewish child to a life of Torah and mitzvos. At this time, the parents must have a clear goal for their child. This will ensure that the Torah being taught to their child from the very beginning will lead him towards that goal.

A person can only be encouraged to study Torah for ulterior motives if his foundations are sound. As long as the original goals were set properly, they can still be reached. However, if the goal set at the beginning was flawed (the desire for honor), the end results could be devastating, since the child is being led astray. Elisha ben Avuyah thus suffered the consequences of his father's wrong intentions.

During the period of the Chanukah saga, *Megillas Antiochus* tells us that the Syrian-Greeks prohibited the Jews from circumcising their children and from keeping Shabbos and Rosh Chodesh. What was so unique about these three mitzvos, that they should have been banned?

One must understand that the Greeks targeted those mitzvos that emphasized the "*sod hahaschalah*," the secret of the beginning. Circumcision marks the first dedication of a Jew's body to Torah and mitzvos. Likewise, Rosh Chodesh marks the dedication of time, the new month, to Hashem, as seen in the mitzvah of *kiddush hachodesh*, the sanctification of the new moon. Shabbos, although coming at the end of the week, is understood to be the source of blessing for the coming week. Thus in the song *Lecha Dodi*, Shabbos is referred to as *mekor haberachah*, "the source of all blessing."[3]

If the Jews could not keep the mitzvos that represented "pure foundations," the Greeks would be successful in their quest to abolish Torah. Without a solid foundation, the Jews could not defend themselves against foreign influences they would encounter later.

Now we can understand the decree mentioned in *Megillas*

---

[3] See *Kedushas Levi, Ki Sissa*; also see *Be'er Moshe, Beshalach* (p. 425) and *Ekev* (p. 257). *Sefer Olas Tamid* cites *Peri Megadim* who explains the expression in the daily Shacharis prayer, "*Hayom yom rishon b'Shabbos*," "Today is a first (second...) day of Shabbos." The implication is that each day receives its unique spiritual sustenance from the previous Shabbos.

Ta'anis: the Greek generals required Jewish maidens to consort with them before being allowed to marry their husbands. By contaminating the beginning of Jewish married life, the Greeks hoped to prevent the growth of Torah, since the Torah's success requires holy beginnings.

The Chanukah miracle reflects the Jews' success in overcoming Greek efforts to contaminate Torah. It allowed them to rededicate themselves to a fresh start built on the principles of "holy beginnings."

Using the principle of *sod hahaschalah*, we can answer another question the commentators ask about the miracle of the menorah: Why was the miracle necessary, since the Talmud (*Yoma* 6b) says that some of the laws concerning spiritual defilement in the Beis Hamikdash are waived if the majority of the community is defiled.[4] Once everything had been defiled by the Greeks, they could have — and should have — used the defiled oil to light the menorah! Why did they risk relying on a miracle by insisting on lighting the menorah with only ritually pure oil?

The answer is that they couldn't rededicate the Beis Hamikdash using contaminated oil. Halachically, it may have been acceptable, but the Jews refused to use anything but pure oil. A dedication requires perfection, and they could only use the purest of oils, with the *kohen gadol*'s seal, for the menorah. With a perfect beginning, they could be assured of continued success.

We can now return to the Talmud's question: *Mai Chanukah?* How does the name "Chanukah" reflect the inner essence of the holiday? The Jews had won the battle against the Greeks; they had used the little flask that lasted miraculously for eight days. Hashem had shown them the *"sod hahaschalah,"* the secret of

---

4 See *Shabbos* 21b.

rededication. This is the essence of Chanukah — dedication — and this best reflects the meaning of the war, the victory, and the celebration.[5]

---

[5] Based on this interpretation we may offer a new reason why the Chanukah menorah is supposed to be lit in the doorway: it alludes to the concept of new beginnings, represented by the entrance to the house.

Reflection on the Last Day of Chanukah

Chanukah celebrates hope in the middle of exile, and light in the middle of darkness

Have you ever noticed how the holiday of Chanukah seems to fly by quicker than any of the other holidays in the Jewish calendar? It always amazes me, and depresses me a bit, to realize on the last night that a week of Chanukah has already gone by.

Part of my reaction is probably a result of the fact that the Chanukah observance doesn't really amount to much. A little longer Shacharis, about ten minutes at the menorah each evening — and that's about it. It's even a regular workday, without any special restrictions. And although there are holiday customs, such as latkes and the dreidel, these are hardly central to the meaning of the holiday.

In fact, no other Jewish holiday observance seems as mundane as Chanukah. If the Chanukah miracle was important enough to underpin a holiday, why didn't the Rabbis give it more substance, like the other holidays?

A few other questions are also in order. The commentaries explain that the name "Chanukah" is a contraction of the words חנו כ״ה, "they camped [and rested from the war] on the twenty-fifth [day of Kislev]" (see *Tur* 670 and *Ran*). It seems rather strange that they would name the holiday after a lull in the war, rather than after the actual victory itself (see *Sifsei Chaim*, vol. 2, p. 3).

The Talmud (*Yoma* 29a) also makes a rather puzzling statement.

> "For the Conductor, upon the early morning light" (*Tehillim* 22:1). Rav Assi said, "Why is Esther compared to the early morning light? Just like the early morning light marks the end of night, the miracle of Esther, too, marks the end of the period of miracles. But there is the miracle of Chanukah [which occurred after the Purim story]? We are referring to miracles that were meant to be written. [The Chanukah story is not mentioned in Tanach.]

This, too, requires explanation. What is the difference between the Chanukah and Purim miracles, that one should be written and read and the other not?

To achieve a better understanding of the holiday, we should have a clear picture of the historical period in which the Chanukah miracle occurred.

During the Chanukah era, the Jews were under the rule of the Syrian-Greek empire. The Greek exile was not like any other exile they had experienced. The Jews were on the soil of the Holy Land, the Beis Hamikdash was standing, and living conditions were bearable. The Greeks appreciated Jewish scholarship and culture; they just wanted the Jews to assimilate Greek culture and ideals into their own. The outlandish Jewish ideals of holiness and spirituality irked the modern Greek sensibility, because they stood in the way of this assimilation.

To further their goals, the Greeks prohibited certain mitzvos, specifically the ones that dealt with the concept of sanctity. Circumcision — representing holiness of the body — and Shabbos and Rosh Chodesh — representing holiness in time — were banned. They disrupted the holiness of Jewish married life by requiring maidens to consort with the Greek generals before their wedding day. The holiness of the Torah itself was marred through a ban on its being taught and its forced translation into Greek (the Septuagint). That was why the Greeks, on entering the Beis Hamikdash, contaminated the holy oil used for the menorah rather than merely destroy it, to show their contempt for holiness.

Unfortunately, the Greeks were quite successful in their attempts. Many Jews, especially among the priests and wealthy upper class, absorbed the Greek influence and became Hellenized. The Beis Hamikdash was defiled by the presence of Greek statues and gods, as some Hellenistic priests looked on approvingly.

Into this glum picture the Maccabees entered. The Maccabees were *kohanim*, the most spiritual tribe of the Jews. They were the most sensitive to the desecration and led a revolt against the Syrian-Greeks. They were joined by a relatively small band of Jews who felt as they did. It was not a pretty sight. Jews were pitted against their own Hellenistic brothers, making it a period of gloom and confusion for the Jewish people.

The small, fearless army of untrained soldiers was phenomenally successful. They won battle after battle, until they seized control of the Beis Hamikdash. They cleaned up the debris and prepared to reinstate the Temple service. Yet only one little flask of holy oil was found, enough to light the menorah for one day. Miraculously, though, the little flask lasted eight days, until they were able to produce new oil.

Although the war lasted another twenty years,[6] by which time four of the five Maccabee brothers would die in battle, the miracle of the menorah proved to be a turning point. It was a ray of hope breaking through the dismal darkness of the exile. The Jews saw that Hashem had not forgotten or abandoned them; eventually they would succeed.

A similar idea is found in the story of Yosef and his brothers, which is always read from the Torah during Chanukah. The Torah (*Bereishis* 37:25) relates that Yosef was sold by his brothers to a caravan that carried spices. Rashi explains the relevance of this fact: usually the caravans would be carrying kerosene and tar, not sweet-smelling spices. However, Hashem did not want Yosef to have to breathe foul-smelling tar on his way to Egypt, so He arranged for him to be sold to spice merchants instead.

The question is obvious. Yosef had just been abandoned and sold by his own flesh and blood. Separated from his beloved father, he had no idea where he was going, what would happen to him, or if he would ever see his family again. It is difficult to imagine a more disillusioning situation. The last thing on his mind would have been the smells around him. Why was it so important for Hashem to arrange this insignificant detail?

---

6 This historical account is based on *Maccabees I* and *II*. See *Chanukah* (Artscroll), p. 33, for discussion about the timing of the Chanukah miracle.

I once saw a treatment of this matter by Rav Mordechai Pogremansky, *zt"l*, the great *gaon* from Telshe, Lithuania. Precisely because Yosef so despaired, the seemingly insignificant detail of the caravan's fragrance provided a small ray of hope. Yosef could not know how things would work out, but he now realized Hashem had not abandoned him. Since his situation was a little more comfortable than he might expect, he knew Hashem was with him. Surely Yosef could count on His future protection, too.

We can now understand why Chazal established Chanukah as a holiday. It is the holiday specifically tailored for the Jew in exile, to offer strength and encouragement, telling us not to lose hope amid the gloom of impending disaster.[7]

This is also why they chose to call the holiday Chanukah, on account of the *"chaniyah,"* the resting from war, rather than the victory of the war. The war was not yet won, and it would still go on for many years. But when they rested from doing battle and kindled the menorah, they felt a surge of optimism and trust that Hashem would yet save and protect the nation. It is this light of hope that the celebration marks.

The Talmud's statement that the Chanukah miracle was not meant to be written can also be understood. Only a complete story is proper to be written. The Purim story fits into this category, and as such was recorded in *Megillas Esther*. The Chanukah story is different. The Jews were still at war and in exile. It was hardly something that could be chronicled. Yet,

---

[7] The Purim story was also an exercise in recognizing Hashem's hidden presence, and as such is also tailored to the Jew in exile. However, whereas the Purim miracle showed Hashem's involvement in the Jewish people's physical survival, Chanukah showed Hashem's involvement in their spiritual survival.

therein lies the essence of Chanukah: it is a story that is still being played out. As long as the Jew remains in exile, he continues to draw hope and inspiration from the Chanukah story, incomplete as it is.

Chanukah's observance reflects this motif. It was meant to be a "mundane" holiday. Set in the regular workweek, it projects a small light surrounded by the mundane reality of the exile. Our goal should be to allow the light and warmth generated by those few minutes of candle-lighting to spread their influence throughout the rest of the day and the year. In the midst of the mundane, the vision of hope must be kept alive.

The Dreidel and Hashem's Chanukah Presence

On Chanukah we recognize Hashem's miracles in the midst of nature

There are many different customs associated with the Jewish holidays. In some cases the source of these customs is logical and meaningful: for example, eating foods fried in oil on Chanukah to recall the miracle of the flask of oil that lasted eight days. Other customs, however, seem to be of doubtful origin, and the commentators try to understand their relevance and meaning. An example is the dreidel, the four-sided Chanukah top with Hebrew letters on each side; dreidel games are played around the world on Chanukah. The origin of the custom of dreidel is not clear, but since Jewish customs are known to have holy sources — even if they seem ordinary or childish — we should try to explore its meaning.[8]

---

[8] The Chasam Sofer would play with a silver dreidel one night each Chanukah to observe the time-honored custom (cited in *Chayim Sheyesh*).

Some suggest that the dreidel was invented at the time of the Greek decrees prohibiting the study of Torah. Jews would teach and study Torah in secret. Should a Greek soldier appear, they would hide their books and pull out tops and play with the children. But a deeper interpretation of the dreidel may be possible.

There are some other questions that must first be raised regarding Chanukah. The Talmud (*Shabbos* 21b) discusses the historical background behind Chanukah: how the Greeks contaminated all the pure oil, and how they found a little flask of pure oil that should have lasted for only one day but instead lasted for eight. The Talmud concludes that the following year the Rabbis declared these eight days as days of praise and thanksgiving. Why did they wait until the following year to establish the holiday rather than doing so right after experiencing the miracle?

The character of the Chanukah celebration seems rather unique. Generally, Jewish holidays are celebrated with rejoicing and festive meals. Even the Rabbinic holiday of Purim is notable for feasting. Chanukah is an exception. The Talmud only mentions that the days of Chanukah are to be days of praise and thanksgiving. No mention is made of feasting. Why is this holiday different from all others?

In the previous chapter we mentioned that the name "Chanukah" is a contraction of the words חנו כ״ה, "they camped [and rested from war] on the twenty-fifth [day of Kislev]." We asked why the name recalls the lull in the fighting instead of the final victory. Let us take a different approach now.

We must first digress for a moment and discuss the role of miracles in general and the Chanukah miracle in particular. The

Ramban (*Shemos* 13:16) explains that there is no real difference between nature and miracles. Hashem's hand guides everything in the world; however, we sometimes are so distracted by mundane events that we fail to see Hashem's hand in them, and instead call it "nature." The purpose of a miracle, which is nothing more than a break from the routine, is to draw our attention to Hashem's control over all areas of life — even the natural. That is why, the Ramban adds, we find many mitzvos in the Torah which commemorate the Exodus from Egypt: to recall the miracles of the Exodus and draw our attention to Hashem's guiding hand in all that happened, and all that continues to happen.

We see from the Ramban that it is human to lose sight of Hashem in the midst of our daily routine. We sometimes need to be reminded to take a step back, so we can better appreciate Hashem's constant involvement in our lives. Rav Simcha Zissel Ziv (*Chochmah U'mussar*, ch. 61) explains the Chanukah miracle in a similar manner. To Hashem, making a little flask of oil burn for eight days is no more difficult than making it burn for one day. In effect, the miracle of the little flask lasting eight days drew our attention to the "miracle" involved in its burning for even one day. It reminded us that what we call "nature" must never be taken for granted.[9]

We can now return to our earlier questions. The holiday was named Chanukah, reflecting the lull in the war, because only then did they have a chance to stop and consider the divine assistance rendered during their battles: something they had not ap-

---

[9] With this principle, Rav Simcha Zissel answers the famous question of the Beis Yosef (670), why is Chanukah celebrated for eight days if the miracle was only for seven, since the flask of oil had enough to burn for one day? The answer is that the eighth day was to serve as a reminder that even when oil burns as it is supposed to, it is also a "miracle."

preciated in the midst of war. Even then, all the nuances were not fully appreciated until the following year, which explains why they waited to establish the holiday. For the same reason, the Rabbis did not include feasting in the Chanukah celebration, to prevent our being distracted from the main purpose of the holiday. They wanted us to have time to reflect on Hashem's miracles and publicize them.

And now we might explain the dreidel. On the sides of the dreidel are the letters *nun, gimel, hei*, and *shin*, representing the words *"Neis gadol hayah sham"* — "A great miracle happened there."

While the dreidel spins, the letters disappear in a blur and are visible only when it comes to a stop. The dreidel represents man — as long as he is immersed in the hustle-bustle of his daily routine, he cannot see the miracles happening all around him. Only when he stops to reflect are his eyes opened to the miracles that were there the whole time. The Chanukah holiday and its customs provide us with valuable lessons, sensitizing us to seeing Hashem throughout the year.

Between Darkness and Light

The distinction between the darkness of Greek culture and the light of Torah

In the opening passages of the Torah, the Midrash (*Bereishis Rabbah* 2:4) perceives a hint of the four exiles of the Jewish people:

> "And the earth was empty" alludes to the Babylonian exile...; "and formless" is a reference to the Persian exile...; "and darkness" is an allusion to the Greek exile [when the Greek government] darkened the eyes of Israel with their decrees...; "upon the face of the abyss" alludes to the Roman exile....

Why did the Rabbis interpret darkness as a referent for the Greek exile? How was darkness the defining characteristic of the Hellenistic culture? Wicked and replete with perversion, perhaps. Heretical and idolatrous, too. But darkness? Ancient Greece was a model of culture, philosophy, and the arts. The Rabbis also recognized Greek culture as a bastion of enlightened wisdom, albeit a forbidden wisdom.[10] What connection, then, is there between darkness and the Greek exile?

The *Mesillas Yesharim* (ch. 3) describes two types of darkness: 1) the darkness of a blind person, which precludes seeing where one is going; and 2) the darkness of dusk, which blurs the vision such that one might see a person as a pole or vice versa. The darkness of dusk is more dangerous than the darkness of the blind, because when one is blind, the dangers are anticipated. The blind person knows to move with caution to avoid stumbling. The visual distortions that come with the darkness of dusk, however, can easily be interpreted as real, since there is sufficient light to see something. The person moving in dusk may not even realize that his vision is impaired and can easily come to harm.

It is regarding the confusion created by dusk that we bless Hashem in the Havdalah service: "Blessed are You, Hashem, King of the Universe, Who distinguishes between light and darkness, between Israel and the nations, between the seventh day and the six days of activity." The distinction, here, between Israel and the nations, and between Shabbos and the weekdays, is a spiritual one, and the ability to appreciate that difference merits mention. But the difference between light and dark is obvious and elementary, so why do we praise Hashem for something so basic?[11] The implication is that a distinction is being made between light and a darkness that could be confused with light.

---

10 See Talmud (*Menachos* 99b), where it is indicated that studying "Greek wisdom" is prohibited because it takes time away from Torah study. Also see *Bava Kamma* 83a, where studying "Greek wisdom" is permitted only for those who are involved with the government.

11 See *Rashi* (*Vayikra* 11:47), which states that *havdalah* (distinguishing) is not necessary when the differences are obvious.

Similarly, the darkness associated with Greece is the darkness that may masquerade as light. The Torah is called "light" (*Mishlei* 6:23) because it instructs us and guides the living of our lives with clarity. The Greeks may have had wisdom, but it was a superficial wisdom that could not offer clear guidance to the soul. Greek wisdom, rather, confused the soul.

The *Megillas Ta'anis* says that when the Torah was translated into Greek, three days of darkness descended upon the world. Perhaps this is because the Torah, translated into Greek, was itself a document of darkness: the true wisdom of Torah lies in the oral traditions, which cannot be captured in translation or on paper.

It took the sharp discerning eyes of the Chashmonaim to recognize the danger of the Greek darkness. The war they waged was a war between the light of Torah knowledge and the darkness of other wisdoms. When the battles were won, the difference became clear. The Rabbis instituted the lighting of the menorah to mark the victory of light over darkness.

Our understanding of the Greek darkness may also explain a rather strange phrase in the Chanukah song, *Ma'oz Tzur*: "*B'nei binah yemei shemonah kav'u shir urenanim*" — "The men of understanding ordained eight days of song and praises." Why does the poet refer to the Rabbis as "*b'nei binah*," men of understanding, rather than using the more common term "*chachomim*," wise scholars?

The word "*binah*" is related to the word "*bein*," meaning between. *Binah* is thus the ability to discern and understand the differences between seemingly similar ideas. The Chashmonaim's virtue, then, was in their ability to distinguish between the subtleties of light and darkness.

The Victory Over Reason

The Greeks tried to break our commitment to the *chukim*

The *Al Hanissim* prayer recited during Chanukah begins: "In the days of Mattisyahu son of Yochanan the *kohen gadol*...when the wicked Greek kingdom rose up against Your people Israel to make them forget Your Torah and to cause them to transgress the statutes (*chukim*) of Your Will...."

The evil decrees of the Greeks are described as causing the Jews to forget the Torah and to transgress the *chukim*, that is, the mitzvos that can't be explained logically. But what, we may ask, is the connection between forgetting the Torah and transgressing the *chukim*? Also, why were the Greeks intent on destroying the *chukim* more than the other mitzvos?

The Ramban (*Vayikra* 16:8) offers a lengthy interpretation of the *se'ir shel Azazel*, the scapegoat thrown down a cliff as part of the Yom Kippur service in the Beis Hamikdash. He concludes his discussion by saying: "In order to properly explain this, it is first necessary to refute the students of nature who follow the Greek philosopher's school of thought that denies anything it cannot comprehend. He and his wicked students arrogantly believe that if they cannot understand something logically, it cannot be true." (Ramban is referring to Aristotle. See Chavel's notes to Mossad Rav Kook ed.)

Greek philosophy could not accept a reality that did not conform to logic. They could not accept the Jews' adherence to *chukim*, mitzvos that defied logic. They were at odds with an otherwise intelligent people that could subscribe to such illogical laws, and they therefore banned their observance. The Greeks reasoned that if the Jews did not keep the *chukim*, the Torah would be forgotten. After all, if somebody observes only what he understands rationally, he is not committing himself to following the word of Hashem, but instead picks and chooses those items that make him feel comfortable. This undermines the whole purpose of Torah, which is to reveal the will of Hashem.

This understanding of Greek philosophy also allows us to explain another difficult midrash. The midrash (*Bereishis* 2:5) describes a Greek decree forcing the Jews to write on the horn of an ox, "We have no part in the God of Israel," Heaven forbid. What was the purpose of this strange decree?

The Maharal (*Ner Mitzvah*, p. 15) explains that the ox horn alluded to the sin of the *eigel*, the golden calf. The Greeks taunted the Jewish people, saying that by sinning with the *eigel* they had forfeited their portion with the God of Israel. This episode needs further explanation. What connection is there between the Greeks and the golden calf?

Elsewhere we have explained that the severity of the sin of the *eigel* lay in their elevating reason and perception above heeding Moshe's orders (see essay "The Atonement beyond Understanding"). Moshe had told the people before climbing the mountain that he would return forty days later. They miscalculated and expected him back one day too early. The *satan* compounded matters by floating an image in the air of Moshe lying dead in a coffin. Rationally, the people concluded that Moshe would not return. They needed something to take Moshe's place, so they built the golden calf. However, they should have placed their faith in Moshe above their own perceptions. The nation failed and fell from its exalted level.

The Greeks capitalized on this past failing. They gleefully reminded the Jews that they had already shown their loss of faith when they elevated human logic over God's Will. They had already fallen from their unique status, and there was no reason for them to continue observing commandments that made no sense. Therefore, they prohibited the Jews from fulfilling the *chukim*.

The celebration of Chanukah is not merely a military victory; rather it is the victory of the total commitment to Hashem over mere reason.

Internal Influence

The different customs of where to light the menorah reflect its influence in both our public and private lives

The Talmud (*Shabbos* 21b) states: There is a mitzvah to place the Chanukah candles in the outside doorway [in order to publicize the Chanukah miracle — Rashi]. If one lives upstairs, he should place the lights in the window, visible to the public. In time of danger, however, the candles may be placed on the table [and the publicizing will be for the people inside].

Rashi explains the danger arose when the gentiles forbade the Jews from lighting candles. Consequently, the *poskim* question the accepted custom in most communities of lighting the Chanukah candles indoors when there is no real danger.[12] The *Aruch Hashulchan* (671:24) justifies the custom, as it would be difficult to light outside given the inclement winter weather of many countries. Although it is possible to enclose the menorah in a glass case (as is done today in Israel) the Rabbis did not want to place a burden on the people.

---

12 Indeed, in Israel today the custom among many people is to light the Chanukah menorah outdoors. See *Mikra'ei Kodesh*, Chanukah, ch. 17.

Perhaps we can offer a different interpretation, based on a thought from the Koznitzer Maggid cited in *Sefas Emes* (Chanukah 5634). The danger referred to by the Talmud may not be physical, but rather the spiritual danger of outside influences.

Rav Elya Meir Bloch, *zt"l*, transplanted the Telshe Yeshivah to Cleveland in 1941, where he had the awesome task of instilling Torah in young Americans who had never experienced the European yeshivah environment. In the 1940s Rav Elya Meir was already a vocal critic of television, although the programs were innocuous by today's standards. He explained his opposition to television by drawing on his own experiences. In the European shtetl the Jew was largely uninfluenced by the outside gentile culture, since he had little contact with that world. The shtetl was a self-contained environment based on Torah.

In America, however, this is not the case. Daily the Jew is confronted by the outside culture—in the workplace, on the streets, etc. The only safe haven of the Jew lies within the walls of his home. There he can close the door and create his own Torah atmosphere. But what happens when television is brought into the home? The very environment he has kept outside is now piped into the living room! That is the danger of television.

When the Jewish community was an insular, well-protected haven with little fear of outside influences, we could afford to place the menorah outside, publicizing the miracle to the outside world and spreading our influence. Over the course of the exile, however, we no longer had that luxury. The winds of negative influence have made their way into the Jewish home.

The primary focus must be on keeping the influence of the miracle indoors, to protect ourselves from outside influences. That is the reason why, even when we publicize the miracle to the outside world, we put the menorah in the window, within the protection of our homes, rather than put it outside as was originally done.

Tu B'Shevat

Teachings of the Trees

The wakening trees on Tu B'Shevat provide a lesson in spiritual growth

The fifteenth day of Shevat, Tu B'Shevat, is called *Rosh Hashanah L'ilanos*, the New Year for Trees. Strictly speaking, this title draws a legal distinction related to the laws of tithing in Eretz Yisrael. Tithes must be separated from any produce grown in Eretz Yisrael before it may be eaten. In a given year, the fruit taken as tithe from one tree may represent the owner's other trees of the same species. However one year's fruit may not be tithe for another year's harvest.

Tradition teaches the new year for fruit begins on the fifteenth of Shevat, because most of the winter rains will have passed and the sap of the new growth has begun to flow: the dormant tree is waking from its winter sleep (*Rashi, Rosh Hashanah 14a*). A tree that blossoms before Tu B'Shevat is considered last year's produce; if it blossoms after Tu B'Shevat, it belongs to the new year.

Other than the day's significance for tithing, there is no

source in the Talmud or Midrash for celebrating Tu B'Shevat. Yet from later sources we find many customs regarding the celebration of Tu B'Shevat: *Magen Avraham* (131:16) cites the practice of eating various fruits; *Likutei Maharich* (vol. 3) describes the custom of dressing in one's Shabbos finery for the new year for trees, because the Torah compares the human being to a tree (*Devarim* 21:19). Let us examine the comparison between man and trees in order to understand the message on Tu B'Shevat for humankind.

The tree goes through cycles in its life. The heavy-laden tree of summer empties itself of fruit in the autumn, and then slowly loses its leaves, one by one. By winter time, the tree stands shorn of its previous glory. For all purposes, it appears to have died. But then comes Tu B'Shevat! In the midst of the cold winter days, when all vegetation seems frozen or dead, the sap of the tree starts to flow beneath the surface bark. Rising slowly from roots buried in the hardened soil, the sap pushes its way up, pumping new life into outstretched branches that reach towards the heavens.

In life, we too often go through cycles of growth. Periods of renewal and growth may alternate with times of stagnation or dormancy. Rav Wolbe, in his *Alei Shur* (vol. 1, p. 34), cites *Sefer HaYashar* that this cycle is part of man's nature. Rav Wolbe adds that a person must not become disillusioned when spiritual growth seems halted; the "low" period will usually be followed by a "high" period that will yield new opportunities for growth.

That is the message of Tu B'Shevat: Even when we feel lethargic, in a rut, and seem to have lost the drive to achieve, we must not despair. Just as winter is an annual hiatus in the life cycle of trees, so bouts of lethargy and unproductivity are necessary phases in the human cycle. Just as with the coming of spring, life-giving sap moves imperceptibly through the trees to branches stretching to the sky, so we too will have renewed energy from deep within our spiritual reservoirs, so long as we set our goal heavenward.

There is another message in the New Year for Trees. Rav Gedaliah Schorr (*Ohr Gedaliah, Shoftim*) points to a difference between trees and annual plants. Although trees require some regular maintenance, they produce fruit each year without any new planting. Plants and vegetables, on the other hand, must be reseeded each year in order to grow.

If a tree is not given proper care, however, it will die. Man, says Rav Schorr, is like the tree. With good maintenance, we need not start over from the very beginning with each goal we set for ourselves. We can build on past accomplishments to go even further. But, as with the tree, we require the proper care to avoid spiritual damage and to grow anew.

Tu B'Shevat inspires us to remember our similarity to the tree. We must be careful to protect ourselves, in order to strive towards greater achievements without having to constantly start over again from scratch.

The Mitzvos of Eretz Yisrael

The rewards for mitzvos performed in Eretz Yisrael are inherent in the mitzvos themselves

Tu B'Shevat has practical application only for Eretz Yisrael, where all produce grown is subject to the laws of *terumos* and *ma'aseros*. These are the tithes given to the *kohen*, the *levi*, and the poor. Tu B'Shevat marks the new year for trees: Any fruit from a tree that blossoms after Tu B'Shevat is considered the new year's produce and cannot be used as tithe for the produce of the previous year.

What is the significance of the agricultural mitzvos associated with the Land of Israel?

Let us examine an interesting dialogue between Hashem and Moshe in the Talmud (*Sotah* 14a):

> Why did Moshe desire to enter Eretz Yisrael? Was he [merely] interested in eating the fruits of the land and enjoying its bounty? Rather, Moshe said [to Hashem], "There are many mitzvos that can only be fulfilled in Eretz Yisrael. I

want to enter the land so I can fulfill all these mitzvos." Hashem responded, "Do you really want anything besides the reward? I will consider it as if you fulfilled them."

How are we to understand Hashem's response? Are we to assume that Moshe's desire to perform mitzvos was for no other reason than the expectation of a reward? The Talmud (*Avos* 1:3) warns quite clearly, "Do not be like servants who serve their master for the sake of receiving reward; instead, be like servants who serve their master not for the sake of receiving a reward." Can it be that Moshe had not reached this level?

We can understand the dialogue with a principle developed by Rav Elya Meir Bloch (*Shiurei Da'as, Bein Yisrael La'Amim*). The *rosh yeshivah* explains that there are two underlying reasons for the observance of mitzvos:

1) As every mitzvah has unique therapeutic value, its observance yields the therapeutic power that corresponds to the mitzvah.

2) Observance of any mitzvah demonstrates our allegiance to Hashem, since it fulfills His commandment. (It makes little difference what the rationale for the commandment may be. Since it is the will of Hashem, our observance proves that we accept His authority.)

Thus we perform mitzvos for two reasons: to derive benefit ourselves, and to comply with Hashem's will. Rav Bloch posits, however, that the therapeutic benefit of the mitzvos can only be derived when residing in Eretz Yisrael.

Based on this understanding, Rav Bloch explains the Sifri (*Devarim* 11:18), who comments that even when the Jewish people are exiled in foreign lands, they must still observe the mitzvos, in order that they know how to observe them when they return to Eretz Yisrael.

What does the Sifri mean? Although the observance of agricultural mitzvos, such as *terumah* and *ma'aser*, is restricted to Eretz Yisrael, there is no such limitation regarding non-agricultural mitzvos. Is it possible that we keep the non-agricultural mitzvos outside of Eretz Yisrael only so that we know how to observe them when we return? What connection is there between the mitzvos and Eretz Yisrael?

Rav Bloch responds that even the non-agricultural mitzvos were meant to be observed in Eretz Yisrael if there is to be therapeutic benefit. Of course the mitzvos must be kept outside of Eretz Yisrael as well, but only to show our allegiance to Hashem. The benefit to be derived from observing mitzvos outside of Eretz Yisrael is that we accustom ourselves to their details, so that we can observe them properly when we return to Israel.

With this observation, Rav Bloch resolves another perplexing matter. Ramban says (*Bereishis* 26:5) that although the forefathers observed all the mitzvos before they were so commanded at Mount Sinai, they only kept them when they were residing in Eretz Yisrael. Thus, Yaakov was able to marry two sisters, because he was living in the house of Lavan, which was located outside of Eretz Yisrael. But if the forefathers were observing all the mitzvos anyway, why did they make a behavioral distinction at those times when they were residing outside of Eretz Yisrael?

The answer is that before the Torah was given, the only reason to perform a mitzvah was for the therapeutic benefit. The observance of a mitzvah before Sinai did not demonstrate allegiance to Hashem, because Hashem had not yet stated the obligation to do so. If, in fact, the therapeutic benefit of mitzvah observance could only be derived in Eretz Yisrael, the forefathers had no reason for keeping mitzvos outside of the Land.

The *Pirkei Avos'* dictum that one should not serve Hashem for the purpose of reward can now be seen in a different light. Serving Hashem for personal benefit only poses a problem when doing so detracts from the higher goal of simply obeying Hashem's authority. However, when a commandment is not applicable — as was the case before Sinai — the primary reason for the mitzvah is the therapeutic gain. Under such circumstances, serving Hashem purely for the mitzvah's reward is perfectly acceptable.

We can now return to the dialogue between Hashem and Moshe. The Jews had not yet entered Eretz Yisrael, and the agricultural mitzvos did not yet apply to them. As such, Hashem informed him, the only reason for Moshe to regret not being able to perform the mitzvos of Eretz Yisrael was for the loss of their therapeutic benefit, their "reward." There was no reason for him to feel that his allegiance was remiss by not fulfilling these mitzvos, since their obligation did not begin until they entered the Land. Given that this was the case, Hashem promised that He would grant Moshe all the therapeutic benefits of the mitzvos, even without his entering Eretz Yisrael.[1]

Perhaps Tu B'Shevat is meant to remind us of the longing we should have to enter Eretz Yisrael and to observe all its mitzvos. May we merit reaping the benefits of the mitzvos of Eretz Yisrael, speedily in our days.

---

[1] See Maharsha (*Sotah* 14a) where he may be alluding to this interpretation.

Purim

Finding the Happy Medium

The days of extremes must be preceded by their opposites in order to create a balance

On the day before Purim, the thirteenth of Adar, it is customary to fast. It is commonly assumed that the fast day, known as Ta'anis Esther, commemorates Queen Esther's orders to Mordechai that the people fast for three days (*Esther* 4:15). However, the commentaries point out that this is not so. In fact, Esther herself fasted in the middle of the month of Nissan. Moreover, *Maseches Sofrim* (ch. 21) cites a custom of fasting to commemorate Esther's fast, on the Monday, Thursday, and Monday after Purim.

The commentaries cite the opinions of Rabbeinu Tam (cited in the *Rosh, Megillah* 2a) and Rav Achai Gaon (*Parashas Vayakhel*). These sources point to the practice of fasting before the Jews went to war with their enemies. The purpose of the fast of Ta'anis Esther is to remind us of their fasting and prayers. (See *Aruch Hashulchan* [686] for further elaboration.)

Perhaps we can offer another explanation for the fast.

Rambam (*Hilchos De'os* 1:3–4) instructs us regarding the dangers of extremes:

> The path of extremes of every character trait is not proper for a person to follow.... The proper path is the middle road of each character trait; the path which is equally distant from each extreme.... A person should therefore not be easy to anger, yet neither should he be cold and unfeeling like a corpse. He should only be angry over something worthwhile to arouse his anger, to prevent it from being repeated. Similarly, one should not lust for anything except for that which the body needs....

Later, in chapter 2, Rambam discusses the therapy for one who finds himself following the extreme:

> What is their cure? A person who has a bad temper is instructed that even if he is cursed or beaten, he should not feel [resentment or anger] at all. He should continue on this path for an extended period of time until he has removed the [tendency towards] anger from his heart.... Then he should return to the middle of the road and continue to follow it for the rest of his days.

Rambam suggests that although the way of extremes is the incorrect path to follow in general, it may sometimes be necessary to temporarily follow an extreme program in order to return to the middle road.

The discussion of extremes leads us to talk about the celebration of Purim. Purim is unique in the Jewish calendar for its mitzvos of excessive rejoicing: consuming a festive meal with wine and liquor, even to the point of intoxication. The Rabbis felt

Finding the Happy Medium

that the great spiritual potential of Purim made the day worthy of such celebration.[1] But that is not to say that the day is without its risks. For that reason, a fast was ordained for the day before Purim. Following Rambam's suggestion, the Rabbis created a middle path, balancing one behavioral extreme with an opposite one. The succession of opposites on two consecutive days keeps the exaggerated behavior of Purim in perspective.

Similarly, Yom Kippur is also a day of extremity.[2] Besides the proscription against all forms of constructive labor, we also deny our physical desires: we don't eat, drink, bathe, or engage in marital relations. Yom Kippur is uniquely so; there is no other day in the Jewish calendar that warrants such excessive self-abnegation.

The Torah and the Rabbis[3] obviously felt that this denial was essential to the experience of atonement on Yom Kippur. But it is important to understand that our conduct on Yom Kippur is not meant as a standard for the rest of the year. Hashem did not intend for us to deny ourselves the pleasures of the world.[4]

For this reason, the Talmud (*Rosh Hashanah* 9a) says that whoever eats and drinks the day before Yom Kippur is considered to have fasted for two days. The commentaries explain that there is an obligation to eat and drink the day before Yom Kip-

---

1 Rav Tzadok Hakohen (*Divrei Sofrim* 14a) posits that on Purim one is capable of totally conquering the *yetzer hara* (evil inclination), thus there is no concern about celebrating excessively.
2 See earlier essay, "Holy, Holy, Holy."
3 Some of the prohibitions of Yom Kippur are Torah law, whereas others are only rabbinic (see *Ritva, Yoma* 73b and *Tosafos, Yoma* 77a). Others hold that all the prohibitions are Torah law (see, for example, *Ran, Yoma* 73b and *Rashi, Shabbos* 114b).
4 See Talmud (*Nedarim* 10a): One who fasts is called a sinner, because he has denied himself the world's pleasures.

pur. Some authorities require a person to eat twice as much as usual, if he is able (*Kaf Hachaim* 604:2 and *Ben Ish Chai, Parashas Vayelech*). In this instance, as well, the excessive demands of Yom Kippur are preceded by opposite excess on the day before. This is done to create a balance and to prevent us from adopting excess as a norm.

We may now have a new appreciation for an enigmatic statement in the *Zohar*. The *Zohar* reads the words "Yom Kippurim" as "Yom Ki-Purim," a day like Purim. What comparison can there be between these two days that seem so different in nature? Both days are marked by excessive behavior: one of indulgence, one of denial. Both days are preceded by days of opposite excess, to ensure that we remain on the middle road of moderation.

A Month of Joy

Purim celebrates the recognition of Hashem's carefully orchestrated masterplan

The Talmud (*Ta'anis* 29a) cites Rav, to the effect that just as the advent of the month of Av signals us to minimize our joy, so the advent of the month of Adar signals us to increase our joy. Simply understood, the statement seems to mean that just as the severity of Tishah B'Av spills over to the rest of the month, so the joy of Purim also spills over. However, this still requires some explanation, for why is the joy of Purim greater than that of Sukkos or any of the other holidays, where no such "spillover" exists?

Furthermore, in the stages leading up to the destruction of the Beis Hamikdash the tragedies escalated — the breaching of the walls of Jerusalem, for instance, and the fighting and killing in Jerusalem proper. We can understand, therefore, why the Rabbis increased the laws of mourning in the days approaching Tishah B'Av. This was not the case in the Purim story. Haman had been hanged eleven months before Purim day. The edict allowing the Jews to defend themselves had been signed shortly thereafter, but the true joy did not come until the Jews were successful in wiping out their enemies on the thirteenth of Adar. There was nothing new that happened between the beginning of the month of Adar and Purim. What purpose is there in celebrating from the beginning of the month?

We must also understand the significance of the name Purim, meaning "lots." When Haman first planned to seek revenge against Mordechai, the Megillah says that he cast lots to determine the most propitious day and month for the extermination of the Jews. The lot fell on the thirteenth day of Adar. Later, the Megillah (9:26) says, "Therefore they called these days 'Purim' because of the lots (*pur*).... " We have already noted elsewhere that the name of something describes its essential nature. The name "Purim" implies that the seemingly insignificant lots played an important part in the story and, by extension, in the nature of the day.

The Purim miracle was unique among biblical miracles because of its lackluster nature. No seas parted; no Heavenly voices were heard; nothing "supernatural" occurred. Seemingly the saga is a series of coincidences: King Achashveirosh became angry at his queen and had her deposed, and Esther "happened" to be chosen as queen, thereby allowing her to intercede on behalf of the Jews. The king's servants plotted to assassinate Achashveirosh, and Mordechai "happened" to overhear their plot and saved the king's life. Mordechai's deed was recorded, yet the king promptly forgot it and only "happened" to remember it the very night Haman entered the king's palace with plans to hang Mordechai. One seeming coincidence after another led to the eventual downfall of Haman and the salvation of the Jews, without any apparent intervention by Hashem.

In truth, however, Purim was as great a miracle as any, but it was a *nes nistar*, a miracle seen as natural, rather than a *nes niglah*, an overt miracle. Haman was blind to Hashem's guiding hand behind every event. He cast lots to calculate the most auspicious time, based on astrological signs, to harm the Jews, thus showing his disbelief in divine providence. But even the casting of the lots was orchestrated by Hashem to fall in the month and on the day that would be beneficial for the Jews (see *Resisei Layla* 10b and 86b).

The holiday is called Purim to remind us that although Hashem's presence and involvement had not been obvious throughout the Purim story, it was there nonetheless — behind every detail, even in something as incidental as the results of the lots, the essence of chance.[5] The Purim story is proof that nothing is a matter of chance; Hashem is constantly watching over everything that happens to His people.

Haman cast two lots: one to calculate the most propitious month and one the day to best destroy the Jews. The joy at the advent of the month celebrates the reversal of fortune from the lots that were drawn to determine the month, and Purim day celebrates the victory from the lots drawn to determine the day. Although Haman had earmarked the month of Adar as a month of destruction for the Jewish people, with Hashem's intervention it actually became a period of joyous celebration. As Hashem's anger, in the month of Av, was visible beyond the day of the destruction of the Beis Hamikdash, Hashem's foiling our enemies' evil designs could be seen beyond the day of Purim itself.

---

5 *Resisei Layla* suggests that the word *pur* is Persian, as it says, "*Hipil pur hu hagoral*" (*Esther* 3:7), for only from the Persian perspective was it chance, and not from the Jewish perspective.

The Torah of Purim

The Purim miracle brought the Jews to a new commitment in following Torah leadership

The Talmud (*Shabbos* 88a) explains the passage describing the giving of the Torah at Mount Sinai, *"Vayisyatzvu b'sachtis hahar,"* "They stood at the foot of the mountain"(*Shemos* 19:17), to mean that Hashem held the mountain over the heads of the Jewish people. He warned them that if they would not accept the Torah they would die. Nonetheless, the Talmud continues, although they had originally accepted the Torah unwillingly, later — in the times of Achashveirosh — they accepted it willingly, as it says, *"Kimu v'kiblu haYehudim,"* "The Jews accepted and received" (*Esther* 9:27) — they now accepted what they had received earlier.

Why does the Talmud say they accepted the Torah grudgingly and had to re-accept it in the days of Achashveirosh? Weren't the Jews praised for their great trust in Hashem when they accepted the Torah without question and said, *"Na'aseh v'nishma"* — "We will do and we will listen"? The *Midrash Tanchuma* (*Noach* 3) explains that *"Na'aseh v'nishma"* only referred to the Written Torah; the Oral Torah was only accepted under duress, as the people feared it would demand too much of them. Only in the days of Achashveirosh did they accept it willingly.

Let us examine this midrash. Why was the Oral Torah so difficult to accept? It seems odd that the Jews needed almost one thousand years before they willingly accepted a major part of the Torah. Furthermore, what was so unique about the Purim story that the people were inspired to re-accept the Torah properly after such a long time?

Michtav M'Eliyahu (vol. 1, p. 75) offers a different slant on the Purim story.[6] When Achashveirosh made his great feast, Mordechai ordered the people not to attend, as they would be led to sin. The Jews, however, felt their absence would anger the king, so they went anyway. Nine uneventful years passed, seeming proof that Mordechai had been wrong. Haman then became prime minister and ordered everyone to bow before him. The Jews discussed the issue and decided to do so, given the circumstances. To justify their behavior, they noted that Yaakov and his sons bowed before Esav, the great-grandfather of Haman. Yet Mordechai would not bow, citing as precedent his own great-grandfather Binyamin, who was not yet born when his brothers bowed to Esav. The people argued that such fanaticism was endangering their lives, yet Mordechai was adamant.

Then the inevitable happened. Haman was so incensed by Mordechai's refusal to bow that he conspired with Achashveirosh to kill all the Jews. Now the people gathered around Mordechai and accused him of endangering their lives. Unmoved, Mordechai said the danger was their own fault, the result of their attending the feast nine years earlier! We can imagine

---

[6] For an extensive elaboration of this theme, see *Return to the Source* (Feldheim, 1984), p. 75.

the Jews' response to such impudence. How dare he lay the blame on them, when Haman's decree was clearly a direct result of Mordechai's obstinacy!

Yet, miraculously, the people accepted Mordechai's reproach. They sincerely regretted their earlier actions and did a complete *teshuvah*. As a result, they saw Haman's carefully laid plans boomerang, and the Jews vanquished their enemies.

We can now try to answer our original questions. The Jews at Mount Sinai were willing to accept the Written Law from Hashem, as it clearly stated what was to be expected of them. The Oral Torah, though, was not as clear. They could not accept that Torah leaders had complete authority to interpret the Torah, even in the face of simple logic, and even if these leaders negated the implications of the Written Torah.[7]

The Purim victory brought the Jews a new appreciation of Torah leadership. Until now they had followed Torah authority when they could understand it, but they had difficulty submitting themselves to Torah leadership when it appeared to be wrong. They could follow such leadership only under threat. The incident with Mordechai, however, changed them. Now the Jews saw how the Torah authority is endowed with insights that go beyond normal logic. Having humbled themselves before Mordechai's words of reproof — illogical as they seemed — they witnessed Haman's overnight downfall, from leadership to the

---

[7] Some classic examples of rabbinic interpretation that contradict the literal Torah are: 1) Regarding injuries the Torah says, "If two people will fight...if there shall be a fatality, you must pay a life for a life; an eye for an eye..." (*Shemos* 21:22–24). The Talmud (*Bava Kamma* 84a) explains that the passage refers to monetary compensation, and not literally to a life or an eye. 2) Regarding tefillin it says, "They shall be ornaments between your eyes" (*Devarim* 6:8). The *Sifri* explains that the tefillin are not placed between the eyes, but rather on the head.

gallows. The people were finally able to follow their Torah leaders willingly, even without understanding their reasoning. This realization was considered so vital to the survival of the Torah that the Rabbis compared it to a new receiving of the Torah. The Purim celebration is more than a mere celebration; it is the culmination of the experience at Mount Sinai.

Amalek and the Power of Lishmah

The intense hatred of Amalek for everything holy can only be countered by battling selflessly for the sake of Hashem

Practically every Jewish child knows the basic Purim story. And yet, although the story of Esther seems deceptively simple, a closer reading of the account reveals many difficulties. We will dwell on one such problem.

After Haman had been put to death and Achashveirosh gave Haman's palace to Mordechai, Esther begged Achashveirosh to have pity upon the Jewish people and allow them to defend themselves against their enemies. Achashveirosh agreed, and the Megillah says (*Esther* 8:10–12):

> He wrote in the name of King Achashveirosh and sealed it with the king's signet ring...that the king permitted the Jews of every city to organize and defend themselves; to destroy, slay, and exterminate the armies of any people or province that threatens them, along with their children and wives, and to take their possessions as booty.

We see clearly that Achashveirosh encouraged the Jews to take all of the spoils for themselves. Yet, shortly afterwards, we find: "The ten sons of Haman were killed, but they did not lay their hands on the spoils..." (*Esther* 9:10).

Later, too, we find: "The Jews who were in Shushan gathered again on the fourteenth day of Adar and slew three hundred men; but they did not lay hands on the spoils" (*Esther* 9:15). And then again in the following passage: "The other Jews in the king's provinces gathered and defended themselves, resting from their enemies and killing 75,000 of their enemies — but they did not lay their hands on the spoils."

Now, since Achashveirosh explicitly permitted the Jews to take the spoils, why did they not do so?

The Purim story must be understood within a larger context. The conflict between Haman and Mordechai was actually the eternal struggle between Amalek and the Jewish people. (Haman was a descendent of Amalek.) Amalek's hatred of the Jewish people was not rooted in a desire for land or material wealth. It was an ideological war, with the goal being the total destruction of the Jewish belief system. Sefas Emes (*Parashas Zachor* 5637) points out that Amalek was willing to sacrifice himself, knowing full well that he would eventually be lost,[8] just to bring the Jewish nation to ruin. Such pure and intense hatred is dangerous because it leaves no room for concession or compromise. That is why the Jewish people are commanded to wipe out the memory of Amalek from beneath the heavens (*Devarim* 25:19). We are also told to keep a vigilant guard against Amalek, constantly re-

---

8   See *Rashi* (*Devarim* 25:18), who compares Amalek to a person who jumps into a scalding tub. Although he may have been seriously burned, he has "cooled" off the water for others. See also *Ha'emek Davar* (*Shemos* 17:14).

membering his evil intentions and past wars, so we might protect ourselves from his diabolical plans (ibid. 17–18).

This may be the explanation for a strange account in the Torah. At the Jewish nation's first encounter with Amalek, Moshe ordered Yehoshua to lead the soldiers in battle. But then the Torah (*Shemos* 17:10–12) relates:

> Moshe, Aharon, and Chur climbed to the top of the hill. And it was when Moshe raised his hand, Israel became stronger, and when he lowered his hand, Amalek became stronger. Moshe's hands grew heavy, so they took a stone and placed it under him and he sat on it....

Why does Moshe raise his hand, when no mention of this practice is made regarding any other war? Also, why should the raising and lowering of Moshe's hand affect the outcome of the battle? The Talmud (*Rosh Hashanah* 29a) explains that when Moshe raised his hand, the people turned their eyes to heaven and were inspired to renew their faith in Hashem. Perhaps the raising and lowering of Moshe's hand served to remind them of their need to be vigilant in their struggle with Amalek. They had to remain connected to Hashem at all times in order to subdue Amalek. As soon as the Jews were distracted even for a moment, as represented by the lowering of Moshe's hand, they would lose ground in their struggle.

How does one do battle with such a dangerous enemy? The pure hatred of Amalek is defeated only through selflessness in serving Hashem. By serving Hashem *lishmah*, for no personal gain, we overcome the perverted selflessness of Amalek.

Now we understand why the people did not take any booty, despite Achashveirosh's express permission. Taking the spoils would have implied a financial motive in fighting Amalek and that the Jews' intentions were less than pure. In fighting Amalek, the Jewish people must be completely dedicated to Hashem to win.

Purim and Seeing beyond Self

The mitzvos of Purim are meant to prevent us from becoming too absorbed in ourselves, like Haman, and to be sensitive to the needs of others

Besides the mitzvos of reading the Megillah and rejoicing on Purim, we have two other mitzvos to perform: *mishlo'ach manos*, the sending of at least two pieces of food to a friend, and *matanos l'evyonim*, gifts of charity to at least two poor people. While *tzedakah* and acts of good will are encouraged throughout the year, the connection between these acts and the holiday of Purim is not clear.

There is a puzzling statement found in the Talmud (*Chullin* 139b) regarding Purim: Where do we find a source for Haman in the Torah? The Talmud points to the verse in *Bereishis* 3:11, where Hashem confronted Adam and Chava after they had eaten from the tree. He asked them, *"Hamin ha'eitz asher tzivisicha levilti achal mimenu achalta?"* — "Have you eaten from the tree that I commanded you not to eat from?" The word *"Hamin"* has the same letters as the word "Haman." What is the connection between eating from the *eitz hada'as* and the story of Haman?

The Talmud may be teaching us a lesson in human nature. The commentators see in Haman the epitome of arrogance and the mindless pursuit of honor (see Rav Chaim Shmulevitz's *Sichos Mussar* 5732–29). Haman had everything a person could possibly want: money, power, family, and prestige. The entire country bowed before him — except for one Jew, Mordechai. Thousands upon thousands of people throughout 127 provinces paid homage to him, yet Haman could find no rest because Mordechai the Jew refused to bow down. He told his wife, "All of this is meaningless to me when I see Mordechai the Jew sitting at the king's gate" (*Esther* 5:13). That, Rav Chaim explains, is the essence of the pursuit of honor. It is all in the imagination. There can be no second best. If he doesn't have everything, he feels he has nothing and can find no pleasure in all that he does have.

"Where do we find a source for such foolishness in the Torah?" the Talmud asks. The answer given is that this attitude is as old as the history of man. Adam and Chava could eat all the delicious fruits in Gan Eden. Only one tree was prohibited: the *eitz hada'as*, the Tree of Knowledge. Why weren't they satisfied? Did they need more? Yet they saw that "the tree was good for eating and that it was a delight for the eyes." Nothing else mattered. They wanted the fruit from that tree, and no other. Such is man; consumed by desire, he cannot think rationally. He thinks only of himself and the present, the same foolishness shown by Haman, who ignored all else because Mordechai refused to bow before him.

The Purim story contains another example of this attitude. Achashveirosh could not sleep one night and asked his advisors to read to him from the chronicles. They read that Mordechai had never been rewarded for saving the king's life. At that moment, Haman happened to enter the king's courtyard, to speak about hanging Mordechai on the gallows. Achashveirosh asked Haman how the king should act toward a man deserving of honor. Haman said to himself, "Who would the king want to honor more than me?" (*Esther* 6:6). It is amazing that it never even entered Haman's mind that the king might want to honor someone other than himself! Again we see how a man can become so self-absorbed that he is totally oblivious to anything else in the world.

Now we might better understand the mitzvos of *mishlo'ach manos* and *matanos l'evyonim*. Chazal wanted to show how self-centered a person could become, as seen in Haman's behavior. This is especially important, when we consider the special mitzvah to celebrate Purim with joyous feasting and the drinking of wine. A person might be so absorbed in his enjoyment that he forgets everything and everyone else. For this reason, Chazal instituted the mitzvos of *mishlo'ach manos* and *matanos l'evyonim* on Purim, to sensitize us to other people's needs and feelings, even as we enjoy ourselves.

With this in mind, we can perhaps offer a new interpretation of another Talmudic statement (*Megillah* 7b): "A person is obligated to imbibe on Purim until he can no longer distinguish between 'Cursed is Haman' and 'Blessed is Mordechai.'" How could the Rabbis condone this type of behavior? Where do we ever find a mitzvah asking us to lose control of our minds?

But our interpretation of *mishlo'ach manos* may show the purpose of the mitzvah of drinking to be the exact opposite of what it implies. The Rabbis instructed us to rejoice by drinking enough alcohol that we become oblivious to the realities of the world ("Cursed be Haman" and "Blessed be Mordechai"). Under such conditions it is difficult to deal with anyone else, let alone empathize with their needs. Yet Chazal wanted to show us that we must never allow our self-indulgence to interfere with our relationships with others. The mitzvos of *mishlo'ach manos* and *matanos l'evyonim* prevent us from falling into the trap of the conceited Haman.

The Four Parshiyos

Parashas Shekalim: United We Stand

Unity serves as an everlasting protection for the Jewish people

The Talmud (*Megillah* 29b) says that on the Shabbos before Rosh Chodesh Adar (or on Shabbos Rosh Chodesh Adar) we read about the obligation to bring the half-shekel. This served as a reminder for everyone to bring their shekalim to the Beis Hamikdash before Rosh Chodesh Nissan when the new collection began. The *Mishnah Berurah* (685:1) adds that today we continue to read this section as a reminder of the half-shekel brought in the times of the Beis Hamikdash. A couple of questions can be asked. Why did the Rabbis need to ordain a special Torah reading to remind people to bring their shekalim? They could have posted signs or sent reminders just as easily. Also, why is the mitzvah of the half-shekel remembered today any more than many other mitzvos performed in the times of the Beis Hamikdash?

The closeness of *Parashas Shekalim* to Purim may indicate a link between the two days. In fact, there is an interesting connection between the half-shekel and Purim. The Talmud (*Megillah* 13b) cites Reish Lakish, who says it was known to the Creator that in the future Haman would pay shekalim to destroy the Jewish people. (Haman offered Achashveirosh ten thousand silver coins to encourage him to wipe out the Jews.) Hashem, therefore, had the shekalim of the Jewish people precede those of Haman, for it is on the first day of Adar that the Jews are told about paying the half-shekel.

What is the connection between the half-shekel and Haman's decree, and how did it prevent the danger?

Some commentators (Be'er Moshe, Sha'arei Aharon, and others) say the significance of each Jew giving a half-shekel — no more, no less — lies in the fact that every Jew is only a half-being and that nobody can fulfill his mission alone. The unique mission of the Jewish people can only be accomplished when there is unity, with each person contributing his own "half" toward the overall "whole."

This is the secret of Jewish success. The Torah was given to the Jewish people only when there was unity, as it says, "*Vayichan sham Yisrael neged hahar*" — "The Israelites camped [singular verb] there, opposite the mountain [Mount Sinai]" (*Shemos* 19:2). Rashi comments on the singular verb "*vayichan*," instead of the plural "*vayachanu*": the Torah tells us that the nation stood at the mountain "like one man, with one heart, in contrast to all the other encampments in the desert which were filled with strife and argument."

Similarly, when there is unity in the Jewish people it strengthens them both spiritually and physically, allowing them to overcome their enemies.

When Haman first broached his plan to Achashveirosh to destroy the Jews, he introduced it by saying, "There is a nation who is scattered and spread throughout the other nations." The commentators (Me'am Lo'ez, Emes V'emunah-Kotzk) explain Haman's words as meaning that there was no reason to fear the Jewish people because there was no unity amongst them.

Hashem ordered the Jews to give half-shekalim to the *mishkan* long before the Purim incident in order to develop a sense of unity in the nation. The unity brought about by the half-shekalim would negate the danger posed by Haman's shekalim and his charges against the Jewish people.

We can now understand why each year, shortly before Purim, we read the section about the shekalim. It was done not only to remind the people to bring their shekalim, but to serve as a reminder to live by the message of the half-shekel. Only by living harmoniously and in unity can we continue to survive as a nation.

Parashas Zachor: Amalek and the Danger of Doubt

The strength of Amalek lies in the weakening of our faith in Hashem's words — and their defeat lies in the strengthening of our faith

Ever since the Jewish people left Egypt, the nation of Amalek has been an enemy of both Hashem and the Jewish people. Amalek first tried to destroy the Jews in the Sinai Desert. Almost a thousand years later, Haman, a direct descendant of Amalek, again tried to annihilate them with the assistance of King Achashveirosh.

On the Shabbos before Purim we read in the Torah about the mitzvah of remembering Amalek. The Torah lays out three mitzvos regarding the nation of Amalek:

1) "Remember what Amalek did to you when you left Egypt." This mitzvah obligates us to read the account in the Torah of Amalek's war with the Jewish people;

Parashas Zachor: Amalek and the Danger of Doubt

2) "Wipe out the memory of Amalek from beneath the heavens." This obligates us to wage war and destroy their entire nation; and

3) "Do not forget [what Amalek did to you]" (*Devarim* 25:17–19).

Rambam (*Sefer Hamitzvos, Aseh* 189) explains that the purpose of these three mitzvos is to arouse our hatred towards Amalek and to keep it aroused forever. It is difficult to understand how the Torah, which usually teaches us to be compassionate and loving, can obligate us to hate anybody so strongly and for such a long time. What is it about Amalek that sets them apart from other enemies of the Jewish people?

The danger of Amalek is clearly not just a physical danger. Had that been the case, it would not have been necessary to destroy their animals and belongings too (see *Shmuel I* 15:2).[1] Furthermore, there would be no reason to read about Amalek today, when Amalek cannot even be identified, let alone pose a physical danger. But what exactly is the spiritual danger that Amalek poses more than anyone else?

We find in Tanach a few confrontations between Amalek and the Jews. In each of these confrontations, Amalek's rise to power was directly influenced by the Jewish people's level of faith in Hashem and the Torah:

1. Shortly after the Jewish people crossed the sea, they camped at Refidim, where there was a shortage of drinking wa-

---

1 There is actually a dispute whether it is necessary to destroy Amalek's property. Rashi (*Devarim* 25:19) says that it is required, as seen by King Shaul. The Rambam, however, does not seem to hold that there is a mitzvah to destroy Amalek's belongings; rather, that Shaul's obligation was unique to his situation. See *Minchas Chinuch* (604).

ter. The people complained to Moshe that it was not worthwhile leaving Egypt to die of thirst in the desert. Hashem ordered Moshe to take his staff and strike a rock, and water would pour forth from it. Moshe followed Hashem's orders and gave the people water to drink. Immediately afterwards the Torah relates (*Shemos* 17:7–13):

> He called the place Massah U'Merivah because of the strife of the Children of Israel and because they tested Hashem saying, "Is Hashem in our midst or not?"
>
> Amalek came and battled Israel in Refidim. Moshe said to Yehoshua, "Choose men for us and go do battle with Amalek; tomorrow I will stand on top of the hill with the staff of Hashem in my hand." Yehoshua followed Moshe's orders to do battle with Amalek; and Moshe, Aharon, and Chur climbed to the top of the hill. And it was when Moshe raised his hand Israel became stronger, and when he lowered his hand Amalek became stronger. Moshe's hands grew heavy, so they took a stone and placed it under him and he sat on it...and his hands were with faith until sunset. Yehoshua weakened Amalek and his people with the edge of the sword.

The midrash (cited by Rashi) explains the juxtaposition of Amalek to Refidim. The reason they were attacked by Amalek was that they questioned Hashem's presence in Refidim. This was also the reason why Moshe had to raise his hands, as the Talmud (*Rosh Hashanah* 29a) explains: "Do Moshe's hands win or lose a war? Rather, when Israel would lift their eyes towards Heaven and subjugate their hearts to their Father in Heaven, they would be victorious; and if not, they would fall."

In other words, since the sin leading to Amalek's attack was doubting Hashem, the victory over Amalek was contingent on the Jews' strengthening their faith in Hashem. That is why Moshe's raised hands are referred to in the Torah as "with faith," because the lifted hands strengthened the people's faith in Hashem (*Be'er Moshe, Beshalach*).

2. Later, in the times of King Shaul, we find:

"Shmuel said to Shaul… 'So said Hashem, "I have remembered what Amalek did to Israel, what he placed for them on the road when they left Egypt." Now go and strike Amalek and destroy everything he has. Have no compassion on him; kill man and woman, infant and suckling; ox and sheep; and camel and donkey' " (*Shmuel I* 15:1–3).

Shaul, however, did not follow his instructions properly: "Shaul and the people took pity on [King] Agag, on the best of the sheep, the cattle…and on all that was good, and they did not want to destroy them" (ibid. 15:9).

Later, he even tried to justify his mistake to Shmuel: "But I did heed the voice of Hashem, and I did walk on the way that Hashem sent me. I brought Agag, king of Amalek, and I destroyed Amalek. The people took sheep and cattle from the spoils…in order to bring offerings to Hashem in Gilgal"(ibid. 20–21).

However, because Hashem's Will had not been carried out properly, Shaul's kingdom was taken away from him.

The Talmud (*Megillah* 13a) says that during the one day that Shaul spared Agag's life until Shmuel killed him, he lived with his wife and she conceived. One descendant from that conception was Haman. Thus we see, again, how the rationalizing and clouding of Hashem's words actually begot the danger of Amalek by preventing their annihilation.

3. In the times of King David, his military general Yoav was again given the order to wipe out Amalek. The Talmud (*Bava Basra* 21a) relates that he killed all the males.

When David chastised him for not killing the females, Yoav answered that the Torah only obligates the killing of the males, as it says: "You should erase the males of Amalek." David, however, replied that Yoav had misread the passage, as it is not read "the males," but rather "the memory."

Again, the proper annihilation of Amalek was blocked by the uncertainty in the Torah transmission.

4. In the Purim story, too, the Midrash (*Esther Rabbah* 7:13) asks, "Why did the Children of Israel of that generation deserve annihilation? Because they enjoyed themselves at Achashveirosh's feast." Although Mordechai, the leader of the generation, had warned the people not to attend (ibid. 7:18), they justified their attendance, saying it was necessary to maintain good relations with Achashveirosh. It was this sin that brought Haman, the descendant of Amalek, to power. Again we see how the scorning of a Torah authority's words granted ascendency to Amalek.

From these incidents we see that doubts in faith are what fueled Amalek, and only through a strengthening in faith can they be defeated. It would seem, then, that the danger of Amalek lies in their ability to plant seeds of doubt in the minds of Jews. It is interesting to note that the numerical value of the word "Amalek" is 240; the same as for the word *safeik*, or "doubt."[2] As long as

---

[2] This may be the understanding of the Talmud's statement, "The best butchers are partners of Amalek" (*Kiddushin* 82a). Rashi explains that sometimes questions arise in the kashrus status of meat, and to prevent financial loss the butcher is tempted to sell it anyway. What does that have to do with Amalek? As explained, though, Amalek's danger is "feeding doubts" to the Jewish people.

doubt lingers in the minds of the Jewish people, their faith and allegiance to Hashem is flawed. The Talmud (*Makos* 24a) says, "Chabakuk came and hinged all of the mitzvos on one central theme, 'The righteous person lives by his faith' (*Chabakuk* 2:4)." Faith is the foundation upon which everything else is built. Without faith in Hashem, the Torah, and Torah leadership, there can be no relationship with Hashem, and ultimately Hashem's authority suffers, as it were (see *Rashi, Shemos* 17:16). The mitzvah to hate and to destroy Amalek is necessary so we can fully accept Hashem's authority without any doubts.

Now we can better appreciate the mitzvah of reading about Amalek, although the nation per se does not exist today. It is important for us to remember the danger of Amalek and how they affected our faith in Hashem. We must always try to eliminate any obstacle that stands in the way of our faith.

Parashas Parah: The Atonement beyond Understanding

The inexplicable *parah adumah* serves as atonement for the sin of rationalization

The section of *Parah Adumah*, the Red Heifer, is read a few weeks before Pesach. During the times of the Beis Hamikdash the reading served as a reminder to those who had become *tamei meis*, ritually contaminated through contact with a human corpse. They were to purify themselves using the *parah adumah* ashes, so they could partake of the *korban Pesach*, the Pesach offering. However, it seems to be more than a mere reminder. The *Shulchan Aruch* (685:7) cites an opinion that this reading is a Torah obligation, not a rabbinic ordinance. Generally, the Torah does not obligate us to set up reminders. Furthermore, since we are still required to read this section today, although the Beis Hamikdash has been destroyed,

Parashas Parah: The Atonement beyond Understanding

it implies a deeper connection between Pesach and the *parah adumah*, one still applicable today. What is the significance of the *parah adumah*?

Parah adumah is first introduced in the Torah (*Bamidbar* 19:1) as a *chok*, a mitzvah which defies reason. Yet, Rashi (ibid. 19:22) cites Rav Moshe Hadarshan that *parah adumah* serves as an atonement for the sin of the golden calf, in the manner that a mother has to clean up the mess her child has left behind. These two statements seem to contradict one another. If the rational explanation for *parah adumah* is to atone for the golden calf, why is it referred to as the classic example of a *chok*? Also how does the purification process for a ritually impure individual atone for the national sin of the golden calf?

To answer these questions let us first understand the reason for *tumas meis*. Rav Tzadok HaKohen (*Machshavos Charutz*, p. 19) explains that when the serpent seduced Chava, and ultimately Adam, to eat from the *eitz hada'as*, death was introduced to the world. The wicked serpent represented the ultimate in impurity; thus its seduction carried with it not only death, but also the spiritual impurity associated with death. We can elaborate on this connection.

Hashem ordered Adam not to eat from the *eitz hada'as* lest he die. The serpent's argument, that by eating the forbidden fruit man would understand good and evil, was both enticing and reasonable. However, Hashem's commandments must be observed even if they do not seem reasonable; they must be observed for no other reason than that they are the will of Hashem. A devoted servant places complete trust in his master, not needing to understand. Adam's sin was that he elevated reason above allegiance to Hashem, and it was this lack of faith that brought death and *tumas meis* to the world.

Almost 2500 years later the Jews stood at Mount Sinai. Hashem offered them the Torah, and they answered, *"Na'aseh v'nishma"* — "We will do and we will hear." The Talmud (*Avodah Zarah* 5a) says that at the time the Jews accepted the Torah, Adam's sin was rectified, and the people were elevated to the spiritual level of man before the sin of the forbidden fruit. They would no longer be subject to death. How did this happen? When the people placed "We will do" before "We will hear," they were in effect accepting Hashem's precepts even before understanding them. They needed to do this in order to rectify the sin of Adam, who put his own reason before Hashem's commandments. They were thus spared the spiritual impurity associated with death.

However, they were not able to maintain this level for long. Forty days after Moshe climbed the mountain to receive the Torah, the people erred grievously. Moshe had told them he would return after forty days, and they miscalculated his return. On the fortieth day the *satan* painted a gloomy picture for the Jews and floated an image before their eyes of Moshe lying dead in a coffin. The people became frightened and clamored to Aharon to build them a golden calf to take Moshe's place. The calf was built, the nation fell from its high spiritual level, and they were once again subject to death and the related spiritual impurity.[3] Why? Because they had failed the same challenge Adam had failed. Instead of trusting Moshe's words, they gave in to their fears and misunderstandings. At Sinai they should have known that true faith in Hashem requires obedience, even when human logic fails.

---

3   See *Nefesh Hachaim* (1:6) for an elaboration of this devastating decline.

Although the option to rectify Adam's sin was no longer available, the Torah still offers a way to cleanse oneself from *tumas meis*: the red heifer. This is the *chok*, the mitzvah that defies logic. How can the same ashes that purify one person (the contaminated person) defile another (the *kohen* preparing the ashes)? It makes no sense — but therein lies its power. The *tumas meis* resulted from putting reason before faith; the purification comes through total commitment to a precept that defies reason, *parah adumah*.

We can now understand Rashi's explanation of *parah adumah*. *Parah adumah* is indeed a *chok*, beyond reason; but because it is a *chok* it is able to atone for the sin of the *eigel*, the golden calf.

Now we can understand the connection between *Parah Adumah* and Pesach. Pesach celebrates our exchanging Egyptian mastery for the mastery of Hashem. *Parah Adumah* serves as a prelude to Pesach. It teaches that in order to be a servant of Hashem, we must make our commitment to His mitzvos go beyond reason or logic.

Parashas Hachodesh: The Gift of Time

Sanctifying the new moon instructs us to maintain control over our time

During the Shabbos before Rosh Chodesh Nissan, we read about the mitzvah of *kiddush hachodesh*, the sanctification of the new moon. This was the first mitzvah given to the Jews as a nation, shortly before they left Egypt. Hashem commanded Moshe, *"Hachodesh hazeh l'chem rosh chodashim"* — "This month [Nissan] shall be for you the beginning of the months." Rashi offers two interpretations for this passage:

1) When the new moon is first seen it should be designated as Rosh Chodesh, the beginning of a new month.

2) The months of the year should be counted from the month of Nissan.

Some explanation is necessary. Why should the mitzvah of sanctifying the new moon be chosen to set the tone for the other mitzvos? Also, why was the month of Nissan singled out to teach us this law? Last, what is so special about this mitzvah that Chazal required us to read it each year?

Seforno on this passage offers a novel interpretation of *kiddush hachodesh*: "This month shall be for you" means that from now on, the months will be yours to do with as you desire, whereas during the days of slavery your days were not your own but rather for the service of others and their desires.

The Jewish people were made responsible for controlling time by sanctifying the new moon. Rather than being controlled by the ordinary time-constraints, the *beis din* (Jewish court) decides when to declare the new month and when to add an additional month.[4] They control the calendar with all its far reaching implications: when the holidays will fall, when a boy or girl reaches majority, and more. This mitzvah gives the Jewish people a mastery, of sorts, over nature itself — truly an awesome responsibility!

Before assuming this responsibility, Jews must fully appreciate the value and importance of time. Seforno at the beginning of the Torah posits that the first thing Hashem created was the concept of time. This implies that time was a prerequisite for all that followed in Creation, since everything in Creation is relative to time. Thus, by granting Israel control over time, Hashem was giving them control over Creation itself.

The custom in Ger was for a bride's father to buy his new son-in-law a gold watch. The Gerrer Rebbe explained this custom by saying it taught the young married couple, as they started life together, that time is golden and must be valued as such.

---

4   In order to synchronize the 354-day lunar calendar with the 365-day solar seasonal calendar, the Torah requires us to add an extra month every few years.

The first mitzvah given to the Jewish people on becoming a nation had them appreciate the value of time and then control it properly. Only then could the other mitzvos be observed, because the mitzvos are all observed within time. Some mitzvos, such as Shabbos, the holidays, and tefillin, are entirely time-bound: they must be performed at certain times. Other mitzvos, although not time-bound, still require us to establish priorities and regulate time — for instance, Torah study and maintaining a kosher home.

A similar idea is echoed in *Koheles* (3:1–8):

> Everything has a season, and there is a time for everything under the heaven. A time to be born and a time to die; a time to plant and a time to uproot that which was planted. A time to kill and a time to heal; a time to break and a time to build. A time to weep and a time to laugh....

Every mitzvah and every emotion has its own designated time. Without an appreciation of that time we cannot fulfill our responsibilities properly.

We can now see the importance of the mitzvah of sanctifying the new moon and why it should be the first mitzvah. It is also quite appropriate for this mitzvah to be given in the month of Nissan, shortly before the Jews were released from slavery, when — as Seforno says — "their days were not their own, but rather for the service of others." Having become an independent nation, they could be entrusted to maintain control over nature and their own time. Accordingly, the Rabbis required us to read the section of *kiddush hachodesh* each year to remind us, as we enter the month of Nissan and the time of our redemption, how we must relate to the precious gift of time.

Pesach

An Educated Freedom

Freedom carries with it the responsibility to make educated choices

Pesach is called *zeman cheiruseinu*, the holiday of our freedom. On a simple level, the holiday recognizes that the Jewish people were released from Egypt after being in bondage for more than two centuries. Of course, gaining independence is reason to rejoice, but it is clearly not the sole reason for the Pesach celebration. In the Torah, whenever we find Hashem telling Moshe to order Pharaoh to free the Children of Israel — "Let My people go!" — it is always followed by another, seemingly contradictory, phrase: "That they may serve Me." (See *Shemos* 7:16, 7:26, 9:1, and 9:13.) If the whole purpose of granting freedom to the nation in slavery was to give them independence, what difference should it make if the people were enslaved to Pharaoh or to Hashem? In neither case would they be completely free. Clearly, there must be more to freedom than is readily apparent.

The Talmud (*Avos* 6:2) offers a rather surprising definition of freedom: *"Ein lecha ben chorin ela mi she'oseik b'talmud Torah"* — "There is no free man like the one who toils in the study of Torah." That seems strange, for what does toiling in Torah have to do with freedom?

True freedom is not merely the absence of slavery, but rather the ability to exercise free will. An uninformed person is not really capable of exercising free will, of making intelligent choices. Only after becoming knowledgeable about the options can a person make an educated decision.

I once had a conversation with a couple, trying to convince them to send their children to a Jewish day school. The mother told me that she would have no problem with her children deciding, on their own, to accept a Torah lifestyle, but she did not think she should force a set of beliefs on her children by sending them to a day school. She said she would rather have them exposed to the public school setting where they would see different beliefs and attitudes. When they grew older, they could make their own decision on how to live their lives.

I asked her what she would do if a doctor asked her advice about a controversial treatment for certain kinds of cancer. How would she respond? Lacking a background in medicine, would she be qualified to offer an opinion? And even if she offered an opinion, would it have any more validity than a wild guess? I pointed out that her children, without a solid day school education, would lack the basic know-how to reach a decision regarding a Torah lifestyle. Although the public school experience might expose them to a broader spectrum of lifestyles, it would not prepare them to properly appreciate their own heritage. Any choice they could make about Torah would be more a guess than an educated decision. Rather than helping her children make decisions, the public school experience would probably cripple them in regard to making real-life Jewish decisions.

The Rabbis understood freedom as meaning the ability to exercise one's free will in making informed decisions. That is only possible if one first toils in Torah, thereby becoming familiar with the options. Accordingly, the goal of Moshe during the Exodus was to lead the Jewish people to Mount Sinai, where they could receive the Torah — and then be able to exercise their free will properly. This, then, is what Hashem meant by "Let My people go, that they may serve Me." As long as they were enslaved to Pharaoh, they could not exercise their free will in worshipping Hashem. And even after they were freed from slavery, they still couldn't render a proper decision regarding Hashem because they could not yet weigh their options. Only after receiving the Torah could they be truly free — that is, able to make an educated decision regarding their service to Hashem.

We celebrate Pesach because it puts us on the right path — the path to receiving the Torah and thereby being able to exercise our free will.

The Taste of Haste

The haste in the Pesach story teaches us how to prevent the yetzer hara from gaining control

The entire holiday of Pesach seems to revolve around the theme of haste. The matzos must be baked quickly to prevent them from becoming *chametz*, "for you departed from the land of Egypt in haste" (*Devarim* 16:3). Similarly, regarding the first Pesach in Egypt, the Torah says: "You shall eat it with your loins girded, shoes on your feet, and with your staff in your hand; you shall eat it in haste; it is a Pesach sacrifice to Hashem" (*Shemos* 12:11).

Why did Hashem find it necessary to arrange the Exodus so that everything had to be done so quickly? What lesson can be learned from the haste of the redemption? Rav Yerucham Levovitz (*Da'as Chochmah U'mussar*, vol. 1, ch. 39) posits that *zerizus*, or zeal, is the key to redemption. What does this mean?

There are different types of slavery from which a person can be redeemed. The Jewish tradition teaches us that the most pathetic slave is the person enslaved to his own desires. A master may control his slave's body, yet have no control over his mind and spirit. One who is unable to control his lusts and desires, however, is enslaved in both body and spirit. Accordingly, the release from this type of slavery is the greatest form of redemption. How can one redeem himself from this enslavement?

The *Mesillas Yesharim* (ch. 6) says that laziness is a major factor in a person's submitting to his desires. In theory, one often knows what should be done and is totally committed to acting accordingly. Yet without the enthusiasm to act correctly, he will think up a myriad of excuses to rationalize his inaction. In order to prevent this occurrence, we must act quickly and not procrastinate for even a short time. Acting with *zerizus* does not allow the *yetzer hara* to rationalize and offer excuses. The *Mesillas Yesharim* warns (ch. 7) that "there is no danger like that of procrastination; every second that one delays creates an opportunity for all types of hindrances." We can now understand Rav Yerucham's insight that *zerizus* is the key to redemption, for it allows us to control the *yetzer hara* and not fall victim to it by rationalizing our inaction: the ultimate slavery.

The Belzer Rebbe would daven relatively quickly. A visitor once asked him why he did not daven slowly like other great rabbis did. The Rebbe replied with a parable. A forest separating two cities was well known as a haven for thieves and wild animals. A merchant from one city once had to travel through the forest to reach the fair in the second city. He hired a carriage and warned the driver to proceed cautiously, to avoid the dangers of the forest. The driver, however, explained that by traveling slowly he would be making the carriage an easy target for the thieves. Better to travel quickly, without stopping, in order to prevent attacks from thieves and animals.

"In a similar vein," the Rebbe explained, "the *yetzer hara* lies in wait, ready to distract our minds during prayer. If a person prays too slowly, he creates more of an opportunity for the *yetzer hara* to enter his mind and make it wander. I feel that when I daven more quickly, there is less chance of my being distracted by the *yetzer hara*, and I can concentrate better."

We can now better appreciate the need for haste during the Exodus. Everything had to be done quickly when leaving Egypt to avoid hindrances, such as the possible concern that the Jews might change their minds and decide to stay in Egypt. Although they had been enslaved and persecuted for 210 years, they might be too frightened to escape into the wilderness and might regret leaving Egypt — as indeed happened several times later on. By acting quickly and departing without even a chance to bake their bread, they wouldn't have an opportunity to change their minds. The key to the Jews' redemption lay in acting quickly, with *zerizus*.

The Exodus thus serves as a lesson on how to deal with one's personal enslavement to his desires; by acting quickly, we do not give the *yetzer hara* a chance to create a point of entry to offer his "wares."

Rav Shlomo Wolbe (*Alei Shur*, vol. 2, p. 389) similarly explains the meaning of the metaphor we often find in the Talmud, where *chametz* is compared to the *yetzer hara*. The main distinction between the baking of matzo and *chametz* is that matzo requires constant working and involvement whereas *chametz* is left to sit: a "procrastination" of sorts, which, as we explained from the *Mesillas Yesharim*, is a major tool of the *yetzer hara*.

The Talmud thus says (*Berachos* 17a): "Rav Alexander would conclude his prayers with the request, 'Master of the Universe! It is known before You that our will is to do Your will, and all that holds us back is the "leavening in the dough." May it be Your will to save us from its hands.' "

Likewise, the *Mechilta* (*Bo* 12:17) reads: " 'You shall guard the matzos.' Do not read 'matzos,' rather 'mitzvos,' to teach that as you guard the matzo from becoming leavened, you must also guard the mitzvos from becoming 'leavened.' If a mitzvah comes to hand, it should be done right away."

The laws of *chametz*, matzo, and the story of Pesach all provide a valuable insight into the workings of the *yetzer hara*. The holiday is a tool given to man, so he can work towards his own personal redemption from slavery to the *yetzer hara*.[1]

---

1 See *Sifsei Chaim* (vol. 2, p. 345) for a similar treatment of *chametz* and matzo.

The Right Appetite

Different mitzvos require different
preparations to perform them properly

On Pesach night we are obligated to eat two different types of food: the Pesach offering itself (in the times of the Beis Hamikdash) and the matzo. According to the Talmud (*Pesachim* 99b), we are prohibited from eating matzo the day before Pesach so that we will have an appetite to eat the matzo at night. It is interesting to note, however, that the opposite is true for the Pesach offering, which must be eaten on a satisfied stomach, at the end of a meal. Rashi (*Pesachim* 70a) explains that the sacrifice must be eaten after the meal so we might better appreciate it.

How can it be that one mitzvah-food must be eaten at the end of the meal, yet the other must be eaten on an empty stomach, both for seemingly similar reasons? It is also not clear how eating the Pesach offering at the end of the meal lets us better appreciate it.

Different mitzvos, even if they share a common feature, require different preparations, depending on the nature and timing of the mitzvah and the people who perform it. For example, regarding the mitzvah of honoring one's parents, the Torah instructs us "*Kabeid es avicha v'es imecha*" — "Honor your father and mother" (*Shemos* 20:12), listing the father before the mother. Concerning the mitzvah of reverence for one's parents, however, we find the exact opposite, as it says "*Ish imo v'aviv tira'u*" — "A person must revere his mother and father" (*Vayikra* 19:3), first mentioning the mother and then the father. The Talmud (*Kiddushin* 30b) explains the reason for the discrepancy. Most people feel a special affinity to the mother, showing her greater honor, because she is softer and more nurturing than the father. The Torah therefore presents the father first, to reinforce the need to honor him equally. On the other hand, it is more natural for children to feel a fear and reverence for their father, because he is usually the stronger disciplinarian. Accordingly, the Torah teaches reverence for the mother first because it requires greater discipline to do so.

Similarly, the Talmud (*Shevuos* 20b) tells us that *zachor v'shamor b'dibur echad ne'emru*, the mitzvos of remembering Shabbos and those of heeding Shabbos were spoken simultaneously. Why was this necessary? "Remembering Shabbos" is a positive commandment, instructing us to think about Shabbos throughout the week by finding special delicacies to honor it.[2] "Heed the Shabbos" is a negative prohibition, a warning not to transgress the laws of Shabbos. For the wealthy person, honoring the Shabbos with beautiful clothes and fine delicacies does not pose any challenge, as he can well afford the greatest luxuries for his Shabbos enjoyment. Refraining from involvement with his many business dealings poses a much greater challenge for him, though. For the poor man, on the other hand, the oppo-

---

2 See Talmud (*Beitzah* 16a).

site is true. It is easy for him to refrain from engaging in business, since he has little to do in any case. However, honoring the Shabbos with the proper delicacies poses a much greater problem, as he does not have much money to spend. Hashem therefore instructed both mitzvos to be performed simultaneously, to give the proper encouragement to each person according to his specific needs.

We may now explain the difference between matzo and the Pesach offering. Basically, matzo is tasteless. Spices may not be added to the matzo, as it is called *lechem oni*, the poor man's bread. It is hard to imagine a person lusting after a piece of matzo; yet Chazal wanted to ensure that the matzos on Seder night be eaten with relish. To accomplish this, they forbade us from eating matzo the entire day before Pesach, hoping that this would excite us and build up an appetite for the matzos.

The Pesach offering is quite different. The meat must be broiled not cooked, because (as *Sefer Hachinuch* points out) broiling meat brings out its full flavor and fragrance as opposed to cooking it in liquid which dilutes the taste. The Torah wants the sacrifice to be enjoyed to the maximum and in a dignified manner. There is no concern that a person might not look forward to eating the broiled meat of the Pesach offering; but there is a different concern. It is important that a person aspire to fulfill the mitzvah for the purpose of serving Hashem and not merely for his own pleasure. Eating a meal before eating the Pesach offering prevents the person from lusting after the meat for his own pleasure, and allows him instead to aspire to fulfill the mitzvah. This is what Rashi alludes to when he says that eating the Pesach after the meal allows us to appreciate it more; not that it will be appreciated more in the physical sense, but rather the mitzvah of eating the Pesach will be valued more.

A similar idea is presented by Tosafos (*Pesachim* 70a), who regard the eating of the Pesach offering at the end of the meal as a fence, to avoid transgressing the Torah prohibition of breaking bones in the sacrificial meat. Generally, a hungry person is likely to eat everything placed before him, even breaking bones to suck out the marrow. A person with a mild appetite eats in a more dignified manner. By eating a meal before eating the Pesach offering, the celebrant will perform the mitzvah in a more refined manner and not break any of the bones.

The different preparations necessary for the matzo and Pesach offering are but another example of how the Torah adjusts mitzvah performance to specific situations, to best accord with and develop human nature.

The Ultimate Victory

Matzo teaches us how to turn an object of derision into one of pride

The celebration of Pesach is perhaps best symbolized by matzo. The eating of matzo reminds us that the Jews left Egypt in such haste, they did not have time to let their bread dough rise. Yet the Haggadah tells us that matzo is the bread of affliction, bread that our forefathers ate in Egypt. The implication is that matzo was food that the Jews ate during the period of Egyptian servitude. Indeed, Ibn Ezra and Avudraham note that it was common for slave owners to feed their slaves matzo, because it was both cheap and filling.

Maharal (*Gevuros Hashem*, ch. 51) asks an obvious question: Why do we celebrate freedom and redemption with a food that reminds us of our enslavement? Imagine a man who has been imprisoned for ten years and who has been fed only dry bread and water during his confinement. He is finally released from jail. His family celebrates with a party. Would they serve dry bread and water to express their joy?

We see an important principle here: True victory does not come merely with vanquishing our enemy. In order to overcome the humiliation we have suffered at their hands, and in order to restore our self-esteem, we must parade the vanquished enemy with pride.

This principle helps us understand a statement in the Talmud (*Megillah* 6a) that in the future (the Messianic era), the princes of Yehudah will study Torah in the theaters and circuses of Edom (Rome). The places which were used for idolatry, immorality, murder, and everything antithetical to Torah will be used as places in which Torah is taught! Will there not be other, more appropriate locations for Torah study in the Messianic era? But as we have suggested, true victory means more than merely conquering the enemy. In the Messianic era, the conversion of institutions once used to mock and scorn Torah into centers for the spreading of Torah will be the ultimate victory.

During the Middle Ages, Jews throughout Europe were forced to wear hats shaped like long cones. (These hats were the forerunner both of dunce caps and witches' hats.) They would be mocked and derided by the ordinary folk for their headwear. But rather than allowing themselves to feel mortified by these ludicrous hats, the Jews found that they could enjoy the fashion. They would take great pride in their identifiably Jewish attire. Jews went on to create styles of clothing that were uniquely theirs, even when it was no longer required by law. This strengthened the pride of the Jews. As they were objectified by others, so their subjective group identity gave them greater cohesion and resolve in the face of adversity.

Moshe Prager, in his *Sparks of Glory* (Mesorah Pub., 1984), relates an incident from the Holocaust:

Everyone in Lublin feared the Nazi Commander Glabochnik, who was notorious for his sadistic cruelty. One day, he herded all the Jews together to the outskirts of the city. He ordered the Jews to sing and dance while his troops beat them savagely. The Jews fell upon one another, trampling each other. Then one Jew freed himself and began to sing:

"Mir vellen zey iberleben, iberleben, iberleben,
Avinu Shebashamayim;
Mir vellen zey iberleben, iberleben, iberleben."

"We shall outlive them, outlive them, outlive them,
Our Father in Heaven;
We shall outlive them, outlive them, outlive them."

The bruised and bleeding mob slowly picked up the refrain and began to sing. Then, as they disentangled themselves, they began to dance. Glabochnik roared with laughter — until he realized that that the Jews were not accommodating him; they were defeating him. He ordered them to stop, but they ignored him. He panicked and pleaded, but they they continued to sing and dance. The SS troops began swinging their clubs and whips and still the singing continued.

Over the course of history the Jews have become expert at turning acts aimed at humiliation into a source of dignity and self-sufficiency. Transforming the symbolic meaning of matzo from one of degradation to one of celebration may have been the first instance of this. We eat matzo with pride — indeed, we experience it as a culinary delight! — impervious to the jibes and ignorance of our enemies. The very food that nourished the Jewish slaves was chosen to be the eternal symbol of our survival. This is both conquest and freedom.

The Miracle of the Sea

What was the real purpose of splitting the sea? Why couldn't Hashem save the Jews in a less obvious manner?

On Pesach we celebrate two major miracles. The first day of Pesach marks the miracle of the plague of the firstborn — every Egyptian firstborn was killed, the Jewish firstborn were all saved, and Pharaoh let the Jews leave Egypt. The seventh day of Pesach commemorates an entirely different event. Six days after the Jews left Egypt, they were panic-stricken. Moshe had led them through the wilderness to camp by the sea. The Egyptians, having changed their minds, were bearing down on them from behind, and the people had nowhere to turn. Then Moshe stretched out his hand over the sea, and a strong wind blew through the night. On the following morning, the sea hardened and split, and the nation crossed over on dry land. Then the Egyptians pursued the Children of Israel into the sea. Again Moshe stretched out his hand, and the sea returned, drowning all the Egyptians. The seventh day of Pesach marks this great miracle.[3]

---

3 Although in the Torah mention of the seventh day of Pesach actually

A logical question can be asked: Why was it necessary to commemorate these two occurrences separately? Why wasn't the miracle at the sea included with the other miracles of the Exodus and commemorated on one Yom Tov?

In addition, the Ohr Hachaim asks a question regarding the miracle at the sea:

The Torah says (*Shemos* 14:27), "And toward morning the sea returned to its power." In a play on words the Midrash (*Bereishis Rabbah* 5:5) reads the word "*le'aysano*" (to its power) as "*li'tena'o*" (according to its condition). This means, according to the Midrash, that Hashem arranged with the sea, at Creation, that one day it would split for the Jewish people. Now the time had come for the sea to fulfill its obligation. The Ohr Hachaim asks why does the Torah allude to Hashem's condition only when the sea returns to its power, rather than when it first splits?[4]

We can answer both of the above questions with an insight I once heard from Rabbi Yehuda Goldberg, a rebbe at the Telshe Alumni Yeshiva in Riverdale, N.Y.[5] The Rambam (*Yesodei HaTorah* 8:1) says:

> The Children of Israel did not believe in Moshe because of the miracles that he performed, for one whose beliefs are based on miracles carries doubts in his heart that perhaps the miracles were the product of magic or sorcery. Rather, all the miracles that Moshe performed were to address a specific need and not merely to prove his supernatural powers.

---

precedes the splitting of the sea, Ibn Ezra (*Shemos* 12:16) explains that the commandment refers to the future events. See *Meshech Chochmah* for a reason why the Torah precedes the event with the commandment.

4 See *Ohr Gedalia Moadim*, p. 148.
5 Published in *Zevach Mishpacha*, vol. 2, p. 287.

When it was necessary to drown the Egyptians, he split the sea and drowned them in it. When there was a need for food, he brought us the manna, etc.

Interestingly, Rambam does not say that the splitting of the sea was needed to save the Jewish people, but rather to destroy their enemies. The implication is that there were other ways the Jewish people might have been spared, but the splitting of the sea was necessary to destroy the Egyptians.

Rabbi Goldberg sees an allusion to Rambam's interpretation in the daily Shacharis prayers after the Shema: "All their firstborn You slew, but Your firstborn, Israel, You redeemed; You split the Sea of Reeds for them — the wicked ones You drowned, and the dear ones You brought across." The order of the prayer seems reversed. It should have stated that You split the sea, brought Your dear ones across, and only then that You drowned the wicked ones, since that was the chronology. Why does it mention the drowning before the crossing of Israel? He posits that since splitting the sea was intended to drown the Egyptians, as explained in Rambam, the order makes sense: "You split the sea in order to drown the wicked ones, and the dear ones You also brought across."

Rambam also implies this interpretation in his commentary on *Avos*. When recounting the different miracles that occurred during the crossing of the sea, he describes (chapter 5:4) the Jews' crossing of the sea as a semi-circle; the nation actually emerged from the sea on the same side that they had entered. If the people did not even cross the sea to the other side, what did they accomplish by going into the sea? The only reason the Jews entered the sea was to entice the Egyptians to follow them, so the water would crash down and drown them. Once that happened, the Jews could emerge from the sea. This accords with Rambam's comment in *Mishneh Torah* that the sea was split to destroy the Egyptians.

With Rambam's idea in mind, we can now return to our original questions. Hashem's pact with the sea concerned not so much its eventual splitting but the return of the waters. The aim was not the journey through the sea but the destruction of the Egyptians. As such, it stands to reason that the allusion to Hashem's pact with the sea occurs in the passages describing the waters returning to their full power and drowning the Egyptians rather than when they first split to let the Jews pass through.

Now we can understand the difference between the first day of Pesach and the seventh. Two types of miracles occurred during the Exodus: those needed to save the Jewish people and those intended to destroy their enemies. The first day of Pesach celebrates the salvation of the Jews, whereas the seventh day celebrates the destruction of their enemies. The Torah did not treat the two celebrations as one because two forms of celebration were needed. The celebration of freedom is joyous, marked by the recital of the complete Hallel. The celebration of our enemies' downfall, on the other hand, is somewhat subdued, as seen in the recital of the half-Hallel. Though we rejoice that the wicked are punished, our joy is somewhat subdued with the realization that human life has been lost.

Expecting the Unexpected

Hashem's assistance often comes from the most unexpected places

On the seventh day of Pesach we celebrate the miracle of the splitting of the sea when the Jews left Egypt. What was unique about this miracle to make it more noteworthy than other miracles occurring during the Exodus? What lesson can we learn from this specific miracle?

In a telling remark, the Talmud (*Sotah* 2a) compares the difficulty of finding one's mate to the splitting of the sea. A similar comment is made in regard to earning one's livelihood, that it is as difficult as splitting the sea (*Pesachim* 118a). What is the connection between the splitting of the Sea, finding a mate, and earning a livelihood?

The great Chassidic master Rav Bunim of Peshischa offers a beautiful explanation. When the Jews reached the sea with the Egyptians in hot pursuit, they realized they were in great trouble — the deep sea cut them off in front, the Egyptians were bearing down from behind, and the dangerous wilderness sprawled on both sides. Probably every Jew had his own idea how Hashem could save them, yet none could have imagined that their salvation would come from the sea splitting before them. Yet that is exactly what happened. The people then understood that Hashem need not send His assistance in the way man imagines. Salvation often comes in the most unusual and unexpected ways.

In marriage, too, people may have preconceived notions about finding the right mate. They think that if they do not take a certain action or frequent a specific place, they will not be able to find their life partner. Yet we are all familiar with stories about couples meeting under the oddest, unimaginable circumstances. That, too, is Hashem working in His mysterious ways. The same is also true with one's employment. People sometimes think they must attend certain schools, move to certain locations, or meet other requirements in order to earn a livelihood. In reality, financial success often comes unexpectedly. Thus the Talmud says the divine assistance that comes to those seeking a spouse and to those seeking a livelihood is similar to the splitting of the sea; there is no way to determine how and from where the assistance will come. Hashem works in ways that are difficult for man to fathom.

The miracle of the sea is celebrated on the seventh day of Pesach because it teaches us an important principle about trusting in Hashem. We must put our faith in Hashem, without stipulating how He must help. Salvation will come as the Almighty sees fit.

Looking at Rav Bunim's interpretation, we can explain another midrash, too. When Yosef revealed his identity to his brothers, he spoke five words to them: *"Ani Yosef, ha'od avi chai?"* — "I am Yosef. Is my father still alive?" The Torah then describes the brothers' reaction: "The brothers could not answer him because they were so astonished before him" (*Bereishis* 45:3). The midrash comments on this:

> Abba Kohen Bardala said, "Woe to the Day of Judgment, Woe to the Day of Retribution. The wise Bilam could not stand up to the chastisement of his donkey...Yosef was from the youngest of the tribes, yet they [the brothers] could not stand up to his chastisement.... How much more so [will we be unable to stand up before Him] when the Holy One will chastise each person according to his actions."

What connection can we find between Yosef's chastising of his brothers, the donkey's words to Bilam, and Hashem's chastisement on the final Day of Judgment? When the brothers were in trouble with the Egyptian ruler, having been accused of theft, they had no idea how matters would work out. They certainly couldn't have imagined that the ruler accusing them would reveal himself as their long-lost brother. This turn of events was so unexpected the brothers were speechless. Similarly, while Bilam rode his donkey enroute to cursing the Children of Israel, the donkey stopped and pinned Bilam against a wall, whereupon he began to beat the donkey. No doubt he wondered about the donkey's unwillingness to move, but the last thing he could have expected was for the donkey to begin speaking! When this happened, Bilam, too, was rendered speechless.

The midrash envisions this happening on the Day of Judgment, too. A person will come to judgment prepared to counter accusations leveled against him for his sins with a litany of mitzvos he has performed. He will be surprised when the prosecution comes from the most unexpected source! The very mitzvos a person uses in his defense will sometimes be turned against him, if they were not done properly and with the right intentions. How embarrassing! It is difficult to imagine the shame and embarrassment one will experience at that time.

We may now be able to explain another puzzling midrash. The midrash (*Tanchuma Nasso* 34 [Buber]) comments on the passage in *Tehillim* (114:3), "The sea saw and fled." What did it see? It saw the bones of Yosef. What does the midrash mean? Perhaps it is saying that the sea saw how man's retribution can come from the most unexpected places, as indeed happened when Yosef revealed his identity to his brothers. It understood that redemption, too, can come in the same manner. The Jew must always be prepared to expect the unexpected.

Sefiras Ha'omer and Lag Ba'omer

Making Days Count

Spiritual growth can only be measured by
small and consistent steps

On the second day of Pesach, in the times of the Beis Hamikdash, there was a mitzvah for the community to bring a barley offering, the omer. The omer is, literally, a type of measure, referring to the amount of barley brought. Beginning that day, the Torah also orders us to count each day and week for seven complete weeks, until Shavuos. This mitzvah is called *sefiras ha'omer*, the counting of the omer.

A few things strike one as being quite strange. First, why is the offering named after the measurement rather than being called by the purpose of the offering? A chocolate cake would not be called a two-tablespoon cake because it calls for two tablespoons of cocoa. Furthermore, what is the significance of counting the days? And what is the connection between the counting of days and the omer offering?

The *Sefer Hachinuch* (mitzvah 306) explains that the counting of the days of *sefirah* is meant to impress upon us the importance of our receiving the Torah. As a person will count down the days and hours until a vacation or some other special occasion, the counting of days until Shavuos intensifies our excitement, our anticipation of receiving the Torah. However, it goes beyond that.

The beginning of the counting was marked, as we saw, by the barley offering in the Beis Hamikdash. The end of the counting was marked by a different offering, the *shtei halechem*, two loaves of wheat bread that were offered in the Beis Hamikdash on Shavuos. The commentators (Abarbanel and others) note that barley is primarily a food for animals (see *Sotah* 14a), whereas wheat is considered a superior grain, most appropriate for man.[1] When the Jewish people first left Egypt they were an undisciplined, somewhat wild nation, comparable to animals. Only when they later accepted the disciplines and moral values of the Torah were they truly considered human.

This elevation was not accomplished quickly. *Avos D'Reb Nasan* (ch. 6) relates an incident about the great Rabbi Akiva, before he began studying Torah. He once saw how dripping water had bored a hole through a large stone. Akiva noted that each droplet of water could hardly have had any effect on the stone, yet slowly the hole was bored. He then reasoned that if soft water could have such an effect on hard stone, how much more so could the hard Torah have an effect on his soft heart — acting slowly, patiently, and persistently. Immediately, Akiva decided to dedicate himself to studying Torah, and from that beginning he grew to become the great Rabbi Akiva.

Spiritual growth can only happen in small increments, and not in huge leaps. Each day must be counted by itself, forcing us to examine our accomplishments and failings and grow a little

---

[1] See *Berachos* 40a, where the Talmud says that wheat contributes to a baby's intellectual development.

bit more. Thus, the counting of days between Pesach and Shavuos is itself part of the development from being animal-like to achieving the level of exalted beings. The cumulative effect of all the counted days is what enabled the Jews to receive the Torah, and that is the purpose of counting the days.

Now we can understand the connection between counting and the omer offering. The omer is a small measure, symbolizing the slow and measured growth of the journey from Egypt to Sinai — growing from being an animal-like people to a nation deserving of the Torah. The counting of each day and week in the omer reminds us of the need to constantly strive towards higher goals, one step at a time, and not to jump too quickly.[2]

According to the above we may begin to understand a difficult midrash (*Vayikra Rabbah* 28:6):

> Rav Yochanan says: Do not take the mitzvah of omer lightly, etc. Rav Levi says that in its merit the Jews were saved in the days of Haman. When Mordechai saw Haman approaching with the king's horse [to honor him in accordance with King Achashveirosh's orders], he thought, "This wicked one must be coming to kill me." His students were studying before him, so he told them, "Flee, lest you get hurt."... [Haman] said to them, "What are you studying?" They replied, "[The laws of] the omer offering that was brought on this day [the second day of Pesach] in the times of the Beis Hamikdash." He asked, "What was this offering brought from, gold or silver?" "From barley," they replied. "How much was brought, ten *kanterin* [a very large measure]?" "It is sufficient to bring

---

2 Rav Shlomo Wolbe finds sources for the idea of different "ladders" for growth in the Talmud, *Rishonim*, and *Acharonim*. (See *Alei Shur*, vol. 1, p. 134.)

ten little pieces," they said. He said to them, "Arise, for your ten pieces have beaten my ten thousand *kanterin* of silver."

What is the link between the omer offering and the Purim victory over Haman? Furthermore, how could the omer offering assist the Jews in their battle against Haman? Since the Beis Hamikdash had already been destroyed, the omer could no longer be offered! However, as noted, the omer represents the slow but measured growth in the days between Pesach and Shavuos, as we strive to attain spiritual perfection. With small yet consistent steps, integrating each day's accomplishments, one can overcome seemingly insurmountable hurdles. Although the Beis Hamikdash was destroyed, the potential for growth during the days of the omer remains. When Haman saw the sudden reversal of his fortune on this day, the second day of Pesach and first day of the omer-counting, he realized that his great position and power could not guarantee his success. The Jews, with their modest efforts towards *teshuvah* and spiritual growth, had overcome all of Haman's carefully laid plans.

The importance of integrating one's spiritual growth is also one of the themes of Lag Ba'omer, the day marking the *yahrzeit* of Rabbi Shimon bar Yochai. The Aruch Hashulchan (*Orach Chaim* 493) adds that Lag Ba'omer was also the day Rabbi Shimon bar Yochai could leave the cave where he had spent twelve years hiding from the Romans. The Talmud (*Shabbos* 33b) relates:

> When they [Rabbi Shimon and his son, Rav Elazar] emerged from the cave, they saw people plowing and sowing seed. [Rabbi Shimon] said, "They put aside eternal life [Torah study] and toil in temporal life?" Wherever they turned their

eyes they sent a consuming fire. A heavenly voice called out to them, "Did you leave [the cave] to destroy My world? Return to the cave!" They returned to the cave for another twelve months. They mused, "The wicked only suffer in Gehinnom for twelve months; surely our sin has been atoned!" The heavenly voice said, "You may leave the cave!"... On *erev Shabbos* they saw an elderly man running in the street carrying two bundles of myrtle branches. They asked him why he was carrying the flowers. "To honor the Shabbos," he replied. "Would it not be sufficient with one bunch?" Rabbi Shimon asked. "One is for the mitzvah 'Remember the Shabbos' and the other is for the mitzvah 'Guard the Shabbos,' " the man said. Rabbi Shimon told his son, "See how precious the mitzvos are to the children of Israel!"

It is hard to imagine what occurred during those last twelve months that allowed Rabbi Shimon to appreciate ordinary activities more than he could after hiding twelve years. Perhaps the great spiritual insights Rabbi Shimon had gained during the twelve years were not yet fully integrated. He was incapable of mastering his own greatness, thus wreaking havoc upon others who had not achieved the same heights.[3]

---

[3] A similar interpretation may be used to explain the gemara (*Sukkah* 28a) regarding Hillel's greatest student, Yonasan ben Uziel. The Talmud describes his greatness: when a bird flew over him while he was studying Torah, it was consumed by fire. The Kotzker Rebbe comments that Hillel himself was so great that the bird flying over him would not be consumed by fire. The ability to contain one's holiness is a sign of spiritual maturity that comes with slow and methodical growth. (Ritva, however, suggests the exact opposite distinction between Hillel and his students.)

In the last twelve months, however, Rabbi Shimon learned to integrate his spiritual accomplishments. He could now recognize greatness in simple activities. The celebration of Lag Ba'omer lets us experience the joy of integrating the ideals of the omer into our lives, through small and measured steps of growth.

A Life of Torah

Lag Ba'omer celebrates the special Jew who devotes his life exclusively to Torah study

The source of the holiday of Lag Ba'omer, the thirty-third day of the omer, is shrouded in mystery. The Talmud does not mention it, yet it is observed by Jewish communities throughout the world. Various reasons are suggested for the celebration:

1. Meiri (*Yevamos* 62b) cites a tradition from the *Gaonim*, that the epidemic that took the lives of Rabbi Akiva's 24,000 students ended on Lag Ba'omer, causing great joy.

2. Aruch Hashulchan (493:90) cites a tradition that Lag Ba'omer is the *yahrzeit* (anniversary of the death) of Rabbi Shimon bar Yochai, one of Rabbi Akiva's five surviving students and author of the *Zohar*. This is why many festivities take place in Meiron, Rabbi Shimon's gravesite. Aruch Hashulchan also says that Rabbi Shimon, who had been forced to hide from the Romans in a cave for twelve years, was able to come out on Lag Ba'omer.

3. The Chasam Sofer (*Yoreh Deah* 233) calculates that on Lag Ba'omer the manna began to fall, and he suggests this may be the reason for the celebration.

The connection to Rabbi Shimon bar Yochai needs to be examined. First, a *yahrzeit* usually has somber overtones. Why is Rabbi Shimon's *yahrzeit* a joyous occasion? *B'nei Yisasschar* (Iyar 3:6) says that many mystical secrets of Torah were revealed to Rabbi Shimon on the day of his death, so we rejoice. But that too must be explained.

In the previous essay we examined the story about Rabbi Shimon's twelve-year stay in the cave. When he came out, he could not fathom how people could forsake the eternal life for involvement with the temporary, physical world. He had to return to the cave for another year, and only then did he view the world in a kinder light.

The Talmud relates that after Rabbi Shimon emerged the second time, he told his son, Rav Elazar, "My son, it is enough for the world that there be you and me." Rashi explains these words, saying that the world could exist solely on Rabbi Shimon and his son's complete devotion to Torah study. We explained what had changed in Rabbi Shimon's outlook during the extra year in the cave. Let us now take a different approach.

The Talmud (*Berachos* 35b) records an interesting dispute:

> "You shall gather grain" (*Devarim* 11:14) — Why must it say this? Since it is written, "This Book of Torah should not leave your mouth; you should contemplate it day and night" (*Yehoshua* 1:8), I might think that it is meant literally. The Torah, therefore, says, "You shall gather your grain," meaning the Torah should accommodate the way of the world [*Rashi* — combine work with Torah study]. Rabbi Shimon bar Yochai challenged, "If a person will plow during the plowing season, plant in the planting season, harvest in the harvest season...what will happen to the Torah? Rather,

when Israel fulfills the will of Hashem, their work will be done by others...." Abaye said many conducted themselves like Rabbi Yishmael and were successful; many did like Rabbi Shimon bar Yochai, and they were not successful.

Nefesh Hachaim (1:8) notes that the Talmud does not summarily reject Rabbi Shimon's opinion; rather it says many could not succeed with such a lifestyle. There is definitely room, and even a necessity, for Rabbi Shimon's doctrine of complete devotion to Torah study, one that excludes any effort in the material world. However, it is only meant for individuals capable of maintaining a certain spiritual level.

Nefesh Hachaim's insight gives us a better understanding of the incident in the cave. After twelve years of uninterrupted study, of subsisting on carobs and water, Rabbi Shimon could not understand anyone needing more than Torah study. Hashem ordered him back to the cave in order to learn the role of the "many," and not focus only on the role of elite individuals. And, indeed, when he emerged, Rabbi Shimon told his son that not everyone was meant to devote himself exclusively to Torah study. It is enough for there to be the few Rabbi Shimons in the world who can ignore everything but Torah study.

On the day of Rabbi Shimon's death, he looked back at his life with great pride. He had dedicated his life to Torah study, without conceding to the needs of the "many." His accomplishment was recognized with great revelations of Torah, which he duly shared with his disciples. Rabbi Shimon's death was not cause for sadness. On the contrary, leaving this physical existence only removed him from the few remaining impediments of this world, allowing him to continue his studies. Rabbi Shimon ordered his disciples to rejoice on his passing, in appreciation of the few individuals capable of this lifestyle.

We may now explain an interesting custom: On Lag Ba'omer we play with bows and arrows.[4] Some suggest that the bow reminds us of the rainbow, which, according to tradition, does not appear in the lifetime of great people. The rainbow was Hashem's sign to Noach that He would not not destroy the world, regardless of the wickedness of man. The great tzaddik, however, protects the world with his own merit, removing the need for the covenant made to Noach. The Jerusalem Talmud (*Berachos* 9:1) says that the rainbow did not appear at all during Rabbi Shimon's life. But this does not really explain why we play with bows and arrows on Lag Ba'omer. However, based on our earlier interpretation, we might say that on Lag Ba'omer we want to express our appreciation for the Rabbi Shimons of the world. The bow reminds us that while most of the world might not attain the spiritual lifestyle of a Rabbi Shimon, we all benefit from him, as his spiritual merit protects the world from Hashem's wrath.

We might now connect the celebration of Rabbi Shimon bar Yochai with the celebration for the manna on Lag Ba'omer. The manna was Hashem's gift to the generation who received the Torah. It was Hashem's way of saying He would never neglect those elevated souls who dedicate their lives exclusively to the study of Torah; their livelihood would come without effort. On Lag Ba'omer we celebrate the supreme effort of the Rabbi Shimons of the world, those who devote their lives to the study of Torah without concern for livelihood, even if their lifestyle cannot be maintained by the majority of people.

---

4 See *Bein Pesach L'Shavuos*, p. 338, for different sources for this custom.

Shavuos

A Time for Torah; a Torah for All Time

The obscurity of the details behind Shavuos emphasize the all-encompassing nature of the Torah

On a Shabbos morning, a little over 3,300 years ago, on a little mountaintop in the Sinai Desert, an event took place that changed the face of the world. Amidst thunder, lightning, and smoke, a nation of over two million people experienced a divine revelation, receiving Hashem's rules for living. Never in history would this experience be repeated. No other nation ever claimed such a fantastic story; yet the Jewish people preserved this collective memory, passing it faithfully from one generation to the next, until today.

Shavuos marks the day of the divine revelation at Mount Sinai. The actual commemoration, however, seems a let-down after the fanfare of the original experience. First of all, the Torah does not even connect the Sinai experience with the celebration of Shavuos. We are merely instructed to count seven weeks from Pesach and then celebrate the following day as a holiday. No reason is given for celebrating this holiday. Although the narrative clearly states that the Torah was given on this day to the Jews, it is odd that the Torah does not clarify this connection. Furthermore, there is no mitzvah on Shavuos commemorating the theme of the day, as there is on other holidays: e.g., the shofar on Rosh Hashanah and matzo on Pesach. It seems as if the Torah tries to divert our attention from the significance of the day. Why should there be such mystery to this holiday?

The answer is that Torah must not be limited in any way. There have always been people who have tried to compartmentalize Torah. Moses Mendelson said, "Be a cosmopolitan man in the streets and a Jew in the home." Others have said, "Torah is fine, but business is business." And yet others have rationalized, "Torah may have been good for the olden times, but today, times are different...."

When Hashem gave the Torah to the Jews, He did not confine it to any specific time or place. The Torah is meant to serve as a guide for every area of life and in all situations: in business as well as in the synagogue, for mundane physical activities as well as rituals.

The Torah did not draw special attention to any specific day or mitzvah celebrating the giving of the Torah, as this might detract from its all-encompassing nature.[1] A Torah celebration cannot be limited to any specific day; every day should celebrate Torah. Likewise, no specific mitzvah can capture the essence of

---

[1] An example of this can be seen in the American celebration of Mother's Day. On one hand, the designation of such a day encourages the highest volume of long-distance telephone calling each year, besides being the busiest visiting day for many nursing homes. On the other hand, the focus on one day also trivializes the honor due one's mother and discourages celebration other days.

Torah, since every mitzvah is an integral part of Torah. Yet there is a day celebrated each year, the anniversary of the Sinai experience, that serves as a catalyst for our reacquainting ourselves with the Torah and for rededicating ourselves to its study. Shavuos is that day.

There is a custom to stay up all night on Shavuos, engrossed in the sweet stirrings of Torah study, to help us reawaken our desire to connect with Hashem's word. The subtle quality of the holiday, coupled with the simplicity of its celebration, exerts a quiet yet powerful force, one drawing the Jew closer to Torah.

Rav Shlomo Wolbe compared Torah study to a thermos bottle. As heat is locked in the thermos, allowing the hot liquid within to be enjoyed later, so the Sinai experience is locked in the Torah, to be re-experienced whenever we study a book of Torah. Shavuos lets us re-experience Sinai to keep it alive throughout the year. We must take advantage of this opportunity!

The Wedding Season

Many of the customs associated with weddings are derived from the giving of the Torah at Mount Sinai

Is there a heart that doesn't throb at the potpourri of conflicting emotions at the Jewish wedding? We have tense moments of anticipation — as the veiled bride is led to her groom, to slowly circle him — leading to solemn and tearful prayers as they stand together under the *chuppah*. The startling sounds of shattering glass give way to the euphoric ecstasy of singing, clapping, and dancing, as the new couple leaves the canopy to share their first moments of privacy. The experience releases a torrent of emotions rarely encountered elsewhere.

The Talmud (*Ta'anis* 26b) calls Shavuos the wedding day between Hashem, the groom as it were, and the Children of Israel, His beloved bride.[2] The nation standing at the foot of Mount Sinai represents the couple standing under the *chuppah*, while

---

[2] This love-relationship between Hashem and the Jewish people is also understood by the Rabbis as being the allegory in *Shir HaShirim*'s romantic dialogue. See *Rambam* (*Hilchos Teshuvah* 10:3).

Hashem's giving the Torah to the Jewish people was the groom giving his bride her wedding ring.[3]

Many customs associated with the Jewish wedding can trace their source to the Sinai experience. The fasting of the bride and groom on the day of the wedding symbolizes the Jewish people's fast on the day they received the Torah (*Tashbatz* 465, as quoted by Rabbi Aryeh Kaplan in *Made in Heaven*, p. 85). The candles accompanying the bride and groom down the aisle remind us of the fire and smoke on the mountaintop. The bride's flowers bring to mind the miraculous blossoming of Mount Sinai before the revelation. The breaking of the glass is said by some commentators to recall Moshe's shattering of the tablets at Sinai (*Sichos HaRan* 96, as cited by Kaplan).

Yet this parallel should be explained a little more fully, so we might better appreciate the celebration of Shavuos.

What distinguishes the marriage from other relationships is its level of commitment. Marriage represents the deepest connection between two parties. The marital knot is so difficult to break — in an emotional, legal, as well as in a spiritual sense — because the husband and wife have invested so much in their commitment to each other. It is this commitment that is celebrated so joyously at the wedding.

Shavuos marks the total commitment between Hashem and the Jewish people. The nation's declaration of *"Na'aseh v'nishma"* ("We will do and we will listen") was a promise to follow Jewish law at all times. The placing of "We will do" before "We will listen" was our commitment to keep the mitzvos under all circumstances, even before we understand their rationale —

---

[3] The comparison of the Torah to the ring can be carried further: as the round ring has no beginning or end, the Torah too is endless.

as the bride pledges her faithfulness to her beloved under all circumstances. And in the same manner as the groom who accepts upon himself to love and cherish his bride forever, Hashem committed Himself not to forsake the Jewish people as His chosen nation for all times, as He said, "You shall be to Me the most beloved treasure of all nations" (*Shemos* 19:5).

We celebrate Shavuos as the anniversary of the original commitment made at Mount Sinai. But it does not only commemorate ancient history; it is a renewal of the original nuptial vows. The word "Shavuos" has the same root as "*shevuah*," or "oath"; each year on Shavuos we renew our nuptial vows to our beloved Creator.

The custom of *tikun leil Shavuos*, engaging in Torah study throughout the night on Shavuos, reenacts the great excitement and love of the wedding night. The "wedding band" of study is admired and cherished, displayed with great pride as a sign of our eternal commitment.

The joy of Shavuos is like the joy of a bride and groom pledging their eternal love and devotion, the wedding season of the Jewish people. Rejoice!

The Power of a Commitment

The commitment at Mount Sinai distinguishes the Jewish people from other nations and distinguishes Shavuos as a holiday

The Midrash (*Eichah Rabbah* 3:2) relates how before offering the Torah to the Jewish people, Hashem first offered it to all of the nations of the world. He approached the Children of Esav and asked them if they would accept the Torah. The Children of Esav asked, "What does it say?" Hashem told them that it says, "You shall not murder." "How can we accept the Torah?" they exclaimed. "Our nation's credo is Yitzchak's blessing, 'You shall live by your sword' (*Bereishis* 27:40); we cannot live without murder!" Hashem then went to the Children of Yishmael and asked if they would accept the Torah. They too asked, "What does it say?" "You shall not steal," Hashem replied. "We cannot live without stealing," they said. "Our inheritance from Avraham is 'His hand will be against everyone, and their hand will be against him' (*Bereishis* 16:12)." Hashem went to

Ammon and Moav to see if they would accept the Torah. "What does it say?" they asked. "You shall not commit adultery." They said, "How can we accept that? Our very being is the result of an incestuous relationship" (*Bereishis* 19:36). Hashem then went to the Children of Israel and asked if they would accept the Torah. "*Na'aseh v'nishma*" — "We will do and we will listen," the Children of Israel responded.

There are some problems with this midrash. First, the three examples given in the midrash are included in the seven Noachide laws incumbent on all people, Jew and non-Jew alike. Why did Hashem ask if they would accept these laws if they were already obligated to heed them? Furthermore, why did these nations respond that they could not live with these rules if they were obligated to follow them anyway?

We can examine these questions using an insight of Rabbeinu Yonah in his commentary on *Avos* (3:12). The Mishnah says that anyone whose good deeds exceed his wisdom, his wisdom will endure. However, anyone whose wisdom exceeds his actions, his wisdom will not endure. Rabbeinu Yonah asks how could somebody's good deeds exceed his wisdom; if he does not know the mitzvos, how could he fulfill them? He answers that it refers to somebody who has agreed to accept the mitzvos fully while he learns more about them. Once a person commits to this extent, it is as if he has fulfilled the mitzvos. Rabbeinu Yonah concludes that this is the meaning of the Jews' response to Hashem, "*Na'aseh v'nishma*"; they agreed to commit themselves now, and to observe everything they would later learn.[4]

We see from Rabbeinu Yonah the power of commitment. A

---

4 Rabbeinu Yonah's principle can actually be found in the *Mechilta* (*Shemos* 12:28).

person can be credited with mitzvos he has not fulfilled by virtue of accepting them. But we can go even further.

Rambam (*Melachim* 8:11) says that the gentile who has accepted the seven Noachide laws, and is careful to heed them, is considered to be of the righteous nations of the world; he merits a portion in the World to Come. While every gentile must heed the seven laws, a person who formally agrees to them is considered a righteous person. Rambam seems to say that not only is commitment comparable to observance, as Rabbeinu Yonah says, it actually raises observance to a higher level. The commitment shows a concern and eagerness to observe the mitzvos that may not be present in the observance itself.

We can now explain the exchange between Hashem and the nations. Although the seven Noachide laws already bound the nations, Hashem wanted them to make a formal vow to fulfill their obligations. Obviously, without a commitment to their current responsibilities, they would not accept the entire Torah. The nations refused. They understood quite clearly that they had no choice other than observing these laws, yet they felt that they could not enthusiastically commit themselves to something so contrary to their nature.

The Jews understood Hashem would not make unreasonable demands. They committed themselves to fulfilling all future requirements, thus showing their eagerness to observe the mitzvos.

The Maharal (*Chidushei Aggados, Shabbos* 88a) uses a similar idea to answer a puzzling question. The Talmud (ibid.) relates that when the Children of Israel said *"Na'aseh v'nishma,"* 600,000 angels appeared and tied two crowns on each Jew's head — one marked *"na'aseh,"* the other *"nishma."* After they sinned with the *eigel*, the golden calf, 1,200,000 angels descended to remove the crowns. Maharal asks why twice as many angels were needed to remove the crowns as to put them on.

When the Jews said *"Na'aseh v'nishma,"* he states, this was equivalent to fulfilling the mitzvos, as Rabbeinu Yonah says, thus linking commitment and observance together. One angel could thus tie two crowns, since they were as one. After the sin, commitment and observance were separated, so another angel was needed to remove the second crown.

The significance of commitment can also be seen in the case of a convert, who becomes a complete Jew by virtue of commitment even before performing any mitzvos. It is noteworthy that the revelation at Sinai appears in the Torah right after the story of Yisro, the first convert, because Yisro's commitment to Torah sheds light on the meaning of the Sinai experience. This may also explain why the story of Ruth, the famous convert, is read on Shavuos. Her words serve to strengthen our own commitment: "Where you go, I shall go; where you lodge, I shall lodge; ...your God is my God, where you die I shall die, and there I shall be buried." It is, therefore, fitting that we read *Megillas Ruth* on the day we celebrate the Jewish people's commitment to Torah.

We can now answer an often-asked question. What is the difference between Shavuos and Simchas Torah, since both holidays celebrate the Torah? Would it not make more sense for Chazal to arrange the Torah reading so it would be completed on Shavuos rather than after Sukkos? But according to our thesis, the holidays celebrate two different themes. Simchas Torah celebrates the Torah itself and the completion of the yearly cycle; Shavuos celebrates the nation's commitment to Torah before it was even given to them.

The Antidote

The Jewish understanding of the *yetzer hara*, and how the Torah helps us conquer it

The Talmud (*Pesachim* 68b) discusses whether or not it is necessary to drink and eat a festive meal on Yom Tov. The dispute is unresolved, but the Talmud says everyone agrees that on Shavuos we are obligated to eat and drink, because on this day the Torah was given. The Talmud does not explain how the giving of the Torah is relevant to eating and drinking. In fact, one might argue that since Shavuos marks the giving of the Torah, it might be proper to spend the day absorbed in spiritual pursuits rather than feasting. What does it mean?

In the previous essay we cited the midrash (*Eichah Rabbah* 3:2) about Hashem offering the Torah to the Jews. He first offered it to the nations of the world — to the Children of Esav, the Children of Yishmael, and Ammon and Moav — who all refused to accept it, claiming their nature is antithetical to Torah observance. Then Hashem offered the Torah to the Children of Israel, who replied, "*Na'aseh v'nishma*."

Hashem's offer to the nations seems a bit of a tease. If the sinful nature of these nations is a part of them, why did Hashem offer them the Torah at all? And what was so praiseworthy about the fact that the Jews accepted the Torah? Perhaps they did not share the disadvantages of the other nations.

Rav Shlomo Wolbe explains[5] that the Jewish understanding of the *yetzer hara*, the evil inclination, differs from that of the other nations. The two approaches can be found in the Talmud (*Bava Basra* 16a). In discussing good and evil with his friends, Job exclaims, "Master of the Universe! You have created the ox with cloven hooves and the donkey with hoofs that are not split. You have created heaven and You have created hell. You have created the righteous and You have created the wicked. Who can impinge upon Your will?" Job believes man's destiny is pre-ordained; he does not control his conduct. Being righteous or wicked, according to Job, involves as little choice by man as might the animal show in choosing its hoof.

Job's friends disagree with him, saying that Hashem created the *yetzer hara*, but He created the Torah as an antidote. Man cannot claim he is powerless against the *yetzer hara*, since he was given the means to overcome it: Torah study. By studying Torah intensely, a person can ward off the lusts and attractions of the *yetzer hara*.

This difference of approach manifests itself in many ways. Some beliefs advocate celibacy and an ascetic lifestyle as a way to defeat man's sinful lusts. Marriage is considered a concession to man's evil nature. This rationale is based on the premise that lust and desire are part of man's nature, and the only way to deal with man's desires is to squelch them or ignore them completely. The problem with this approach is that it leaves a person with no way to combat the *yetzer hara*, for someone who denies his physical

---

5 I heard this in Yeshivas Be'er Yaakov, summer 1979.

drives will ultimately destroy himself. The Torah's approach is different. Marriage and enjoying life's pleasures are actually encouraged. Fortified with Torah, a man can face his desires and control them; he uses them properly rather than ignore them.[6]

The nations could not understand how they could accept the Torah, because it seemed to be contrary to their very nature. The Jews, however, understood that Hashem would not make impossible demands. They willingly accepted the Torah to be able to overcome the *yetzer hara*.

Now we understand why it is a mitzvah to eat and drink on Shavuos. It is the Torah, given on Shavuos, that enables us to enjoy the physical pleasures of this world, since it provides us with the means to deal with our instinctive drives.

---

6 See *Kiddushin* 30b.

A Torah of Chesed

The central theme in the Torah is chesed, and that is the character trait needed for the Messianic era

On Shavuos we celebrate the giving of the Torah at Mount Sinai. It is unique among Jewish holidays in that it has no special mitzvah linked to it. Although the Torah mentions the mitzvah of *shtei halechem*, the offering of two loaves of wheat bread brought in the Beis Hamikdash on Shavuos, after the destruction of the Beis Hamikdash there is no mitzvah observed in conjunction with Shavuos.

However, it is interesting to note that right after mentioning Shavuos, while discussing the holidays and their respective mitzvos, the Torah mentions a mitzvah lacking a clear connection to Shavuos. The Torah says: "When you reap the harvest of your land, you shall not remove completely the corners of your field as you reap, and you shall not gather the gleanings of your harvest; you shall leave them for the poor and for the proselyte" (*Vayikra* 23:21–22).

What do the gifts for the poor have to do with Shavuos? Perhaps this may allude to Rabbi Akiva's comment on the passage "*Ve'ahavta lerei'acha kamocha*" — "Love your neighbor as yourself" (*Vayikra* 19:18). *Toras Kohanim* quotes Rabbi Akiva, who says that *"Zeh klal gadol baTorah"* — "This is a central principle in the Torah." On the day we celebrate the Torah, it is fitting to discuss the central mitzvah of showing care and concern for others. It may also allude to the assemblage at Mount Sinai, about which the Torah says, *"Vayichan sham Yisrael neged hahar"* — "Israel camped at the foot of the mountain"(*Shemos* 19:2). Rashi comments on the use of the singular form of the verb "camped": *"K'ish echad b'lev echad"* — "like one man, with one heart."

The nation achieved a level of unity at Mount Sinai that had not been achieved elsewhere. Unity among the Jewish people was a prerequisite to their receiving the Torah. The mitzvah of sharing with the poor helps unify the nation as one.

In truth, the Talmud (*Sotah* 14a) relates that *chesed* (kindness) plays a prominent part in both the beginning and end of the Torah. In the beginning we find that Hashem made garments of skin for Adam and Chava to clothe them. At the end of the Torah we find Hashem involved with Moshe's burial. Rav Yerucham Levovitz (*Da'as Chachmah U'mussar*, vol. 1, p. 174) explains that if the beginning and end of the Torah portray *chesed*, it means that the whole Torah is a Torah of *chesed*. The mitzvah of *chesed* may thus very well be the mitzvah of Shavuos.

We may now offer a reason for reading the *Book of Ruth* on Shavuos. The Midrash (*Yalkut Shimoni* 601) comments, "This megillah has neither laws of ritual impurity nor laws of prohibition; so why was it written? To teach the reward for those who perform *chesed*." It is fitting that on the day we celebrate the giving of the Torah of kindness, we read the megillah that was written solely to teach the reward for kindness.

The midrash, though, is puzzling. Where do we see a focus on *chesed* in the story of Ruth?

The story of Ruth is actually the story of the roots of King David and the Messianic dynasty, her descendants.[7] How did this Moabite princess merit such greatness?

Our forefather Avraham is known to represent the attribute of *chesed*. It was he who instilled this character trait into the nature of the Jewish people. However, Avraham's descendants, the Jewish people, could not achieve their final goal of forming a dynasty worthy of leading the world into the Messianic era until they could develop their innate trait of kindness into a complete kingdom of *chesed*.

Although Avraham was the embodiment of *chesed*, there were certain "sparks" of *chesed* lodged in Lot, his nephew. Lot had absorbed these sparks from the house of Avraham, but when he distanced himself from Avraham and moved to Sodom (*Bereishis* 13:11), the sparks of *chesed* left with him, and they became distorted. These sparks would have to be reclaimed and reunited with Avraham's family to complete the development of *chesed* before the founding of the Messianic dynasty through King David.

Lot continued to practice *chesed* in Sodom, endangering his life in a society that was the antithesis of *chesed*.[8] The Midrash (*Bereishis Rabbah* 41:4) thus says, " 'I have found David my servant' (*Tehillim* 89:21) — where did I find him? In Sodom." Yet Lot's choice of environment contaminated his *chesed*,[9] and the

---

7   The following is based primarily on *Maharal* (*Netzach Yisrael*, ch. 32), on a lecture by R' Uziel Milevsky, *zt"l*, of Yeshivas Ohr Somayach, and on *Mema'amkim, Parashas Vayera*.

8   See *Pirkei d'Reb Eliezer* (25) and *Sanhedrin* (109a, b).

9   As seen by Lot's offer to hand over his daughters to the violent mob

sparks were transmitted to his children, Ammon and Moav.

Since Lot's descendants inherited his *chesed*, the Torah chastises them for not feeding the Jewish people who passed through the lands of Ammon and Moav while trekking through the desert: "They did not greet you with bread and water on the road when you left Egypt..." (*Devarim* 24:6). We have no record of any other nation offering food to the Jewish people, but more is expected of Ammon and Moav; they should have followed their ancestor's example. Because they did not display this trait, no Ammonite or Moabite male could ever marry into the Jewish people (*Devarim* 23:4–7).

The story of Ruth begins with Elimelech, a leader of the Jewish people, betraying his people in time of need. There was a famine throughout Israel, and while Elimelech's family had more than enough food, he moved with his wife and two sons to the fields of Moab to avoid helping his brethren. The Midrash (*Ruth Rabbah* 2:5) traces the name Elimelech to the words "*Eilay savo malchus*," "The monarchy shall come to me," because he was a descendent of Yehudah. Yet Elimelech would not know monarchy because he lacked the necessary trait of *chesed* towards his brethren.

A son of Elimelech, Machlon, married the Moabite princess Ruth, and his brother Kilyon married Orpah, another Moabitess. Soon both brothers died, but Ruth refused to desert her mother-in-law, so she followed her, penniless, back to Israel. Humbly she gleaned in the fields to support her mother-in-law and herself, thus showing a kindly nature, unlike the Moabites. Ruth had inherited the trait of *chesed* from her ancestor Lot, and she proved herself worthy of rejoining Lot's *chesed* with that of Avraham.

---

rather than hand over his guests (*Bereishis* 19:8).

For these two chains of *chesed* to merge, the union had to occur through an act of *yibum*, the levirate marriage — thus Ruth married Boaz, her deceased husband's cousin. *Yibum* assures continuity and brings satisfaction to the deceased and is therefore considered to be the highest form of *chesed*.[10] (See *Rashi, Bereishis* 48:29 — the *chesed* done with the deceased is the truest *chesed*.)

This, then, is the meaning of the midrash. The purpose of the *Book of Ruth* is to trace the Messianic dynasty to its source, the *chesed* in Lot's family. The *chesed* that Ruth practiced with her mother-in-law and deceased husband caused her to become the great-grandmother of King David and the eventual Mashiach.

Therefore, it is more than coincidence that the *yahrzeit* of King David is observed on Shavuos. How fitting that the person who was the product of the two lines of *chesed* should be remembered on the day marking the giving of the Torah of *chesed*!

---

10 *Yibum* involves marrying the widow of one's brother. The child from the *yibum* relationship bears the soul of the deceased; the practice is thus considered a *chesed*, as it gurantees continuity for the soul of the deceased. Although technically Boaz's marriage to Ruth was not *yibum* since he was not a brother, it was, nonetheless, able to accomplish similar results (see *Ramban, Bereishis* 38:8). It is interesting to note that King David's lineage from Yehudah was also the product of an act of *yibum* between Yehudah and Tamar (see *Bereishis* 38).

Tishah B'Av

Tishah B'Av and the Fast Days

The stages of a loss: the different fast days all serve to emphasize the loss of the Beis Hamikdash

Four fast days during the year recall the destruction of the Beis Hamikdash in Jerusalem. Asarah B'Teves (the tenth day of Teves) marks the beginning of the Babylonian siege of Jerusalem. Shiv'ah Asar B'Tamuz (the seventeenth day of Tamuz) commemorates the breaching of Jerusalem's walls. Tishah B'Av (the ninth day of Av) marks the actual destruction of the Beis Hamikdash (both the First and Second Temples). Tzom Gedalia, on the third day of Tishrei, commemorates the death of Gedalia ben Achikam, the righteous governor of Jerusalem, shortly after the destruction of the first Beis Hamikdash.

Although we can understand why the Rabbis would decree a fast commemorating the destruction of the Beis Hamikdash, it is more difficult to understand why so many other fast days were ordained. When a person passes away, his *yahrzeit* is observed on the day of his death. The day when the person first took ill, or when he was first taken to surgery, or when he was buried, are not marked by observances because they are all secondary to the passing. Here, too, the siege around Jerusalem, the breaching of the walls, and the death of Gedalia seem secondary to the destruction of the Beis Hamikdash. Why should we commemorate them independently?

This question can be answered by means of a parable I once heard from Rabbi Ya'akov Haber of Monsey, N.Y., in response to a young person contemplating intermarriage.

Imagine seeing an important-looking person guarding a tightly locked box. Surrounded by bodyguards, he leaves an office building. The man enters an armored limousine and is driven off, followed by an armed escort. Suddenly the limousine is blocked by a car, and a group of masked men jump out. They yell for the box to be given up, and they begin to shoot at the limousine. As the bodyguards return fire, the important-looking man jumps from the limousine holding the box and runs down the street. A few blocks further on another group starts chasing the man, trying to grab the prized box. Again, he is able to fend them off and escape. The once-important-looking man now looks a bit bedraggled, yet he still clings to the box with his remaining strength. This scene repeats itself a few more times, but the man is able to dodge his pursuers and keep hold of his cherished possession. Finally, totally worn out, the man enters a forest, digs a hole, and carefully places the box in the hole. After cautiously covering the hole, the man leaves the forest.

Upon imagining this scene played out, we can't help wondering what was in the box. What object was so important that it attracted so much attention? Why was the man so willing to endanger himself for it? Now imagine that you gave in to curiosity and dug up the box, broke the lock, and carefully opened the inside packaging. Imagine your surprise at finding a plain glass vase with a label on the bottom: "Wal-Mart, $1.99"!

We now have two choices. One response could be, "A plain vase? That's all? What a waste!" And the vase is then tossed aside. Another, more intelligent response would be, "I can't understand why so many people would want a simple vase, or why the owner would take such pains to protect it. But since it does mean so much, I must be missing something. Let me examine the vase again or have it analyzed in a laboratory."

The young person contemplating intermarriage does not see much value in Torah, but the fact that so many Jews throughout the ages were willing to guard it from their many antagonists shows that it must have value. Perhaps he or she lacks the knowledge to appreciate that value. Rather than just tossing it away by marrying out of the faith, it would be wiser to examine it again, carefully, to try to understand that value.

The destruction of the Beis Hamikdash was the greatest tragedy to befall the Jewish people in its history. However, centuries later, it is hard for us to appreciate the gravity of the event. We fail to see the meaning in mere mortar and stone.

So the Rabbis decreed fast days, not only for the day of destruction of the Beis Hamikdash, but also for the events before and after. These may have been secondary events, but the Rabbis were so devastated that they marked each step with a fast day, letting us pause and reflect. If we don't understand the tragedy, the problem is with us. The fast days serve as reminders; we must examine the tragedy of the destruction of the Beis Hamikdash again and again, so we might begin to appreciate the immensity of the loss.

The Limitations of Mourning

Throughout time all Jewish tragedies are remembered on Tishah B'Av

Tishah B'Av is definitely the saddest day of the year, marking not only the destruction of the two Batei Mikdash but other historical tragedies as well. The Talmud (*Ta'anis* 26b) tells of three other tragedies occurring on this day: 1) The spies returned from Canaan with a bad report, whereupon Hashem decreed that the entire generation would not enter the land; 2) Betar, a major city, was destroyed only sixty years after the second Beis Hamikdash fell; and 3) the Romans plowed up the site of the Beis Hamikdash.

Later historic misfortunes are also commemorated on Tishah B'Av, including the Crusades in 1096 and the Jewish expulsion from Spain in 1492. Recent rabbinic leaders have even composed Tishah B'Av liturgies to mark the Holocaust.[1] Why was this one day — Tishah B'Av — chosen to commemorate all the *Yiddishe*

---

1   See Artscroll's *Complete Tishah B'Av Service* (p. 382) for *kinnos* authored by the late Bobover Rebbe, *zt"l*, and Rav Shimon Schwab, *zt"l*.

tzorres (troubles) occurring throughout history? Why shouldn't each tragedy have its own time for mourning?

On a trip to Israel I visited an amazing little Holocaust museum called *Marteif Hashoah*, Chamber of the Holocaust, built in a cave on Mount Zion. I had never seen so many pieces of desecrated *sifrei Torah* and other artifacts from the camps. Outside the cave was a stone-floored patio surrounded by walls filled with little plaques. Each plaque held the name of a Jewish community in Europe and the date that community was destroyed during the war. Many names were new to me, but some I recognized from the yeshivos that bore their names: Slabodka, Telz, Ponovezh, Mir. Others held the names of great Chassidic courts: Ger, Vizhnitz, Belz. Hundreds of plaques stared quietly from the walls, memorializing hundreds of shtetlach and millions of Jews lost to the world.

It struck me that the dates on those plaques could probably fill every day of the calendar with the *yahrzeit* of some shtetl or other. The loss of every shtetl was a tragedy of great proportion. Yet if each *yahrzeit* were marked, every day of the year would be a Memorial Day. This couldn't be!

I thought about the custom whereby everyone attending a funeral washes his hands afterwards, before entering a house. Moreover, it is customary not to dry one's hands, but rather to shake off the excess water. Rav Samson Rafael Hirsch (cited in *Concern for the Living* [Targum Press, 1990], pp. 74–75) explains the custom, saying it helps us "wash away" thoughts of the past and the deceased, allowing us to turn our thoughts to present and future needs. Yet our hands are not dried, to remind us that we must carry a bit of the past with us, to guide us in meeting our responsibilities.

If we were to put all our energy into remembering what once was, we could never move forward, for we would be lost in the morass of the past. Our focus must be on the future; what does Hashem want us to achieve? We reflect on the past and its losses only to help us move toward our goals.

Chazal chose Tishah B'Av, the source of many of our *tzorres*, as the day to commemorate Jewish suffering. We have an opportunity to reflect on our losses; but we then carry those images with us, as we spend the rest of the year trying to reclaim and rebuild our heritage. Only a nation that understands its past can look forward to a brighter future. Tishah B'Av is not merely a day focusing on the past; it is also about the future.

Mourning the Loss of Reality

The destruction of the Beis Hamikdash was more than the loss of a building: we have lost a way to appreciate reality

Small clusters of people sit crouched on the floor in stocking feet. Low strains of muffled voices add to the gloom. It is the familiar picture of a traditional Jewish family mourning the loss of a loved one.

One day each year, this emotionally charged scene is reenacted in shuls around the world. Tishah B'Av is the national day of mourning, marking the loss of the two Batei Mikdash in Jerusalem — first over 2,400 years ago and then 1,900 years ago.

It is hard to imagine why the Rabbis required the same observance for both types of mourning. Can our mourning for stones and mortar match the grief of a bereft family? The question is perhaps more relevant as we view a beautiful modern Jerusalem. How do we begin to understand the words of the *Nachem* prayer recited Tishah B'Av afternoon, where we mourn the "ruined, scorned, and desolate city"?

Let us examine two different forms of existence, the spiritual and the physical. The physical world is often said to represent the "real world," while the spiritual world seems remote and abstract. The Torah, however, teaches the opposite. The spiritual world is as "real" as the physical — even more so, as it is the eternal essence of all life, whereas the physical world is temporary. In fact, we regard the physical as a mere reflection of the spiritual world.[2]

The nature of spiritual reality can be seen in the law of *temurah*, the prohibition against transferring holiness from one consecrated animal to another. The Torah says that if a person dedicates an animal to the Beis Hamikdash and then tries to transfer the sanctity to a different animal — even to a better animal — both animals are holy, and the person also receives lashes (*Vayikra* 27:10). Why does the Torah deal so harshly with this person, who only wished to upgrade his gift by bringing a better animal for sacrifice?

The *Sefer Hachinuch* (Mitzvah 352) explains that the Torah wants to impress upon us the seriousness involved in creating holiness. Once consecrated, an article's sanctity cannot be removed at will. On the contrary, should a person try to retract the holiness, rather than disappearing it will spread to the second animal as well.

When people perceive holiness as something abstract, it is not governed by the laws of the physical world. Accordingly, it should be easy to change holiness as you desire. The Torah, how-

---

[2] See *Shiurei Da'as* (p. 38, American ed.) for an elaboration of this concept. As an example he cites the term "to grow," used to describe physical maturation; the real concept of growth, however, refers to spiritual maturation. The physical concept of growth is merely a manifestation of the spiritual concept.

ever, teaches that spirituality is real; when one consecrates an animal, it undergoes a real change, one that remains.

We must understand that concepts of *kedushah* (holiness) and *taharah* (ritual purity) are as real as molecular biology; and *tumah* (spiritual pollution) is as much a concern as germs and bacteria. The fact that spiritual components cannot be dissected or observed in a petri dish does not undermine their existence.

The Beis Hamikdash exemplified the world of spirit. The daily miracles occurring in the Beis Hamikdash clearly showed an aspect of life that modern man is unaccustomed to seeing. Contrasts between Jerusalem and other cities, between Jew and gentile, between Shabbos and weekday, were not merely conceptual — they were actually felt and seen.

With the destruction of the Beis Hamikdash these distinctions blurred. People no longer felt the reality of the spiritual world as clearly as before. They replaced the inner dimension of life with the physical laws of nature and science. Spirituality became religious theology.

The beauty of Jerusalem does not lie in its breathtaking landscapes or clear blue skies. There may very well be other cities with grander terrain. Its true beauty lies in its spiritual "clothes." When Jerusalem is denied its spiritual uniqueness, when its holiness is ignored, it is no different from any other city. It could very well be described as a "city of desolation and ruin" amidst the bustling streets and skyscrapers.

Similarly, Jew and gentile may share physical characteristics; it is in the spiritual makeup that there is a distinction. When the Jew ignores his spiritual side, assimilation and intermarriage are foregone conclusions. A person can hardly be blamed for keeping an abstract, distant ideal from interfering with "true" love.

Only if one realizes that spiritual differences between Jew and gentile are real and palpable, can he understand that the two cannot be joined in a successful marriage.

Tishah B'Av does not merely mark the loss of an ancient building. It mourns the loss of an entire dimension of existence. We mark this spiritual tragedy as we mark a physical tragedy, letting it remind us of the void in our lives. Yet how can the Rabbis expect a twenty-first-century Jew to mourn the loss of something he never experienced?

I once heard of an event that occurred when the Western Wall was liberated in 1967. Word spread that the Old City of Jerusalem was again in Israeli hands, and the soldiers pressed forward eagerly towards the wall. There was an outpouring of emotion as they caressed and kissed the wall that had not been seen for nineteen years.

Two soldiers, however, were products of the extremely secular Shomer Hatzair movement. They seemed totally unmoved by the emotion. One turned to the other and asked, "Why are they all crying? It's only a wall!"

The second soldier shrugged his shoulders. But then he, too, began to sob.

The first soldier was incredulous and asked, "So why are you crying?"

He replied, "I'm crying because I don't know why they are crying...."

Our mourning on Tishah B'Av may not necessarily represent an honest appreciation of the great spiritual loss we suffered in the destruction of the Beis Hamikdash. We have become so empty of spiritual content that we don't even know what we're missing. But that itself may be reason enough for mourning.

The Yom Tov of Tishah B'Av

Tishah B'Av draws us close to Hashem by enabling us to recognize our distance from Him

The weeks following Tishah B'Av are called the *sheva d'nechemta*, the seven weeks of consolation. During these weeks, the haftaros that are read offer the Jewish people words of consolation from the *navi* (prophet) Yeshayahu. These weeks seem to serve as a bridge, connecting Tishah B'Av to the Yamim Noraim, the High Holidays. What is the connection between these days that are so different in character?

The *navi* Yirmiyahu calls Tishah B'Av a *mo'ed*, or holiday (*Eichah* 1:15).[3] This raises yet another question: Why would Tishah B'Av, a day devoted to mourning Jewish tragedies, be considered a holiday?

Rav Yerucham Levovitz, *zt"l*,[4] says that the word *mo'ed* refers

---

3 For this reason, the *Shulchan Aruch* (559:4) rules that the *Tachanun* prayer, always omitted on holidays, should not be said on Tishah B'Av.
4 Quoted and explained by Rav Shlomo Wolbe in *Alei Shur* (vol. 1, p. 115) and in *Larachok V'Lakarov* (Be'er Ya'akov, 1978).

to a meeting place, as in the *ohel mo'ed*, the Tent of Meeting in the Tabernacle. The holidays, then, provide an opportunity for the Jewish people to "meet" and renew their relationship with Hashem.

How is such renewal achieved? A relationship may be given new life either through greater togetherness or through enforced separation. We know that in a healthy, working marriage, couples vacation together to enjoy each other's company. These times of companionship strengthen their relationship.

However, in a marriage where there is discord and stress, couples may decide to separate temporarily. Such separation may engender longing and renewed appreciation of each for the other. Here, separation aids the restoration of healthiness and joy to the partnership. Husband and wife reunite, or meet, with their love and concern for each other strengthened and given new vigor.

Hashem's relationship with the Jewish people has often been compared to the union between husband and wife.[5] The need for togetherness, as well as separation, may similarly apply.

When the Jews observe the mitzvos properly, their relationship with Hashem is healthy and vital: The *mo'ed* during which Hashem and the people meet and the Jews celebrate in His presence, strengthens their union with Him.

Historically, we "vacationed together" within Hashem's presence in the Beis Hamikdash, during Pesach, Shavuos, and Sukkos. However, as our relationship with Hashem had grown stale, He also was no longer interested in our company. He allowed the Beis Hamikdash to be destroyed. The *mo'ed* then served to help us reconnect with Hashem, through the experience of alienation from Him.

---

5   See earlier essay, "The Wedding Season."

A great chasm has opened before us with the loss of the Beis Hamikdash, and in the long *galus* that envelopes us we long to reunite with Hashem. Absence makes the heart grow much fonder. And so, Tishah B'Av is a *mo'ed*, a meeting through separation, a separation that leads to meeting.

This discussion helps us answer another question: Why is the month of Cheshvan called Mar-Cheshvan, or "the bitter month of Cheshvan"? *Sefer Hatoda'ah* suggests that Cheshvan is the only month lacking a holiday and is thus considered bitter. But once again, the resolution of one question raises another: Why would a month with no holidays be more bitter than those months which include fast days, such as Tamuz and Av? There may be no days of special joy in Cheshvan, but neither is there the hardship and physical deprivation of fasting.

But, as we have explained, the fast days, as with the festive days, provide the opportunity to connect — or reconnect — with Hashem, if not through closeness then through the perceived absence of Hashem's presence, which brings about a longing for closeness. Only the month of Cheshvan, with no festive or fast days, leaves us without the opportunity to reach out to Hashem, and so we remain bitter and alone.

We can now appreciate the bridge between Tishah B'Av and Rosh Hashanah. Only when we recognize what is lacking in our relationship with Hashem can we pray for the restoration of His Kingdom. This is the major theme of the Rosh Hashanah prayers. It is thus fitting that Tishah B'Av initiates the preparations for the High Holidays.

The Art of Loving Every Jew

Some practical suggestions on how to love others who don't share our own lifestyle or beliefs

The Talmud (*Yoma* 9b) says the first Beis Hamikdash was destroyed because the Jews violated the Torah's three cardinal sins: idolatry, adultery, and murder. The second Beis Hamikdash, however, was destroyed because of *sinas chinam*, unwarranted hatred. This teaches us, the Talmud concludes, that unwarranted hatred is as serious as the three cardinal sins.

More specifically, the Talmud (*Gittin* 56b) says the second Beis Hamikdash fell because of an incident involving Kamtza and Bar Kamtza. It tells of a host who publicly humiliated his mistakenly invited guest, Bar Kamtza. Angered, Bar Kamtza slandered the Jewish people to the Roman Caesar, initiating a chain of events that led to the destruction of Jerusalem. Maharsha comments that this story was merely one example of the petty divisiveness evident at the time preceding the destruction. It is interesting that the Talmud's example of *sinas chinam* involves an insensitivity towards the feelings of someone as wicked as Bar Kamtza. Since even this type of *sinas chinam* led to the destruction of the Beis Hamikdash, we must try to understand the requirements of respecting and loving our fellow Jews, to rectify history's mistakes.

The Torah says, *"Ve'ahavta lerei'acha kamocha"* — "You shall love your neighbor as yourself" (*Vayikra* 19:18). Rabbi Akiva considers this mitzvah the central principle of the Torah (*Sifra*). Rabbi Akiva experienced the reality of this mitzvah personally. His 24,000 students — the hope of the Jewish people following the destruction of the second Beis Hamikdash — lost their lives in a plague during the period of *sefiras ha'omer*. The Talmud (*Yevamos* 62b) says they died because they were remiss, to some extent, in honoring one another. The Jews were deprived of Torah leadership and scholarship because of a lack of *ahavas Yisrael*.

Similarly, the sage Hillel was once approached by a gentile who wanted to learn the whole Torah while standing on one foot (*Shabbos* 31a). He wanted to understand the central theme of the Torah before converting to Judaism (*Maharsha*). Hillel replied, "What is spiteful to you, don't do to your friend; that is the Torah. The rest is merely commentary." Rashi sees this as the essence of both the interpersonal mitzvos and the ritual mitzvos, too. The essence of the Torah lies in our recognizing a significant other — whether it is an ordinary Jew with his everyday needs or the Creator Himself placing obligations on His people.

Yet despite the prominence accorded this mitzvah, *ahavas Yisrael* seems as alien today as it was thousands of years ago. Clearly, if the Beis Hamikdash is not yet rebuilt, *sinas chinam* has not been eradicated from our midst. Some of the inconsiderate behavior we encounter is clearly a result of underdeveloped *middos* (character traits). However, much of what seems a lack of *ahavas Yisrael* may stem from an inability to properly express one's true sentiments.

Ahavas Yisrael, like many other mitzvos, is an acquired skill. Of course, the halachic limits (to whom the mitzvah does and does not apply, and what falls within its category) must be studied before it can be put into practice. But the feeling of love and concern for a fellow Jew and how that feeling is expressed must be developed.

This is especially important when we deal with Jews who may not share our lifestyle or live according to our halachic standards. People often distrust those who behave differently. Although there may truly be a concern for the other party, we may have difficulty expressing our concern in a way that promotes *ahavas Yisrael*.

Here are a few ideas I have found helpful in developing the art of loving each Jew, especially when dealing with *ba'alei teshuvah* and those who have not yet made a full commitment to following the mitzvos.

1. Love must be felt by both parties in a relationship. A person must know and feel that the other person reciprocates that concern — not only for his *neshamah* and future in the World to Come, but for the person, just as he is today. A love that is not conveyed to the other party, regardless of the many claims to the contrary, cannot be called a true love. Imagine a spouse who claims to love his partner. If the partner does not feel that love, can it really be classified as such?

Even when the other person's actions or beliefs are unacceptable, if there is a genuine feeling of concern and respect expressed, it will be recognized and appreciated.

Rav Shimon Schwab once related an incident from his early years as a student in the Mir Yeshiva in Poland. He planned to visit his parents' home in Frankfurt for Pesach. As was customary, he approached the *mashgiach*, Rav Yerucham Levovitz, for a loan to buy a train ticket. Upon returning after Pesach, he went to the *mashgiach* to repay the loan, and he thanked him. Rav Yerucham chastised him, "Does etiquette take precedence over halachah? Aren't you familiar with the prohibition of *ribbis devarim?*"(Thanking a lender may sometimes constitute a prohibited form of paying interest.)[6]

The following year, Rav Schwab again approached the *mashgiach* for a loan. This time, however, when he returned, he repaid the loan without saying a word. Again Rav Yerucham chastised him, "Is there no *hakaras hatov* (appreciation)?"

Rav Schwab was perturbed. "When I said thank you I was chastised, and when I did not say it I was chastised. What am I supposed to do?"

Rav Yerucham answered him, "It may be true that the halachah does not allow you to thank me, but the feelings of *hakaras hatov* should be so strong, that I should be able to see you struggling not to verbalize it. I don't see that struggle!"

True *ahavas Yisrael* should be seen and felt — through body language, tone, and expression, even if one's actions are limited by halachah.

2. A person's efforts should be recognized and appreciated, even if the results don't measure up to one's standards. Change doesn't come easily for anybody. Surely we would like to see ev-

---

[6] See *Yoreh Deah* 160; *Igros Moshe, Yoreh Deah*, 1:80.

ery Jew achieve a full level of Torah observance, but it doesn't always happen. The changes that are made, however, must be acknowledged. Perhaps the effort it takes for one person to accept half a mitzvah is much greater than the effort most people show in keeping all the mitzvos.

Most people would be proud of not speaking *lashon hara* for an hour — despite the fact that they may not exercise care the rest of the day. Shouldn't credit be given, then, to a person who has begun to keep kosher at home, yet still eats at non-kosher restaurants?

The Kotzker Rebbe once asked his chassidim, "If two people are on a ladder, one on the second rung and one on the ninth, who is higher?" The chassidim looked at each other in amazement. Obviously the person on the higher rung was higher! The Rebbe, however, answered differently. "It depends in which direction the two people are headed. If the person on the bottom is climbing up, and the one on top is climbing down, although it may appear that the one on top is higher, the reality is the opposite. In a matter of moments they will have passed each other and the bottom person will remain higher."

As long as a Jew is ascending, he must be appreciated and loved for his efforts, while being encouraged to grow further.

David R., a student of mine, had family problems and was unable to maintain a kosher home. He confided to me, rather proudly, that while the food wasn't kosher, he did wait six hours between eating meat and milk. I wasn't sure how to respond. True, he was making a sacrifice in doing what he could, but halachically it was worthless. (There is no additional prohibition in eating non-kosher meat with milk.)[7]

---

7   See *Yoreh Deah* 87:3 and *Dagul MeRevava*, ad loc.

I then recalled a *Rashi* in Chumash. In the section of *nedarim* (*Bamidbar* 30:6), Rashi refers to a situation in which a woman vowed to abstain from certain foods. Her husband annulled the vow without informing her. The woman, not knowing about her husband's action, transgressed her vow. Although she had not actually transgressed, since her vow was annulled, the Torah still required her to atone for the sin. Why? In reality, the woman may not have sinned, but she felt she had violated her vow. Her resistance to sin had been lessened, enabling her to sin more easily next time. She required atonement, to prevent her from becoming desensitized.

The same was true with David R. Although no mitzvah was being performed, in his mind he was making a sacrifice to fulfill the will of Hashem. Hopefully, this victory would allow him to make other sacrifices and perform other mitzvos properly. It was important for me to acknowledge his accomplishment.

Care should be taken, though, that the acknowledgment not be misconstrued as compromising one's own ideals, but rather an appreciation of a positive step in the right direction. It must be understood that notwithstanding one's personal challenges and victories, great as they may be, the Torah's standard does not change.

3. The intrinsic value of every Jew must be appreciated, merely by virtue of his being a Jew. Part of the mitzvah of loving a fellow Jew is to emulate the love of Hashem for the Jewish people.[8] Hashem's love for the Jewish people is unconditional.[9] Even when He must punish the Jewish people, His love for them

---

8   See Rabbi S. R. Hirsch in Horeb, pp. 359–360; also *Ilana D'Chaya* quoted in *Memaynos Netzach* on *Parashas Kedoshim*.
9   See *Pri Tzaddik* (*Yisro* 41) in the name of the Yud Hakadosh.

remains unwaveringly strong. Our love for one another must also be unconditional.

The Ba'al Shem Tov[10] understands the passage "Love your neighbor as yourself" to mean that as a person loves himself, although familiar with his own shortcomings, he must likewise love his fellow Jew, despite recognizing his failings and shortcomings.

Siblings may constantly bicker and squabble about everything, yet in a healthy family, the depth of their love for one another will rarely be affected. Their feeling is not based on the other's actions or beliefs; rather, it is an inherent love. They can accept each other as they are, not as they would like them to be. Likewise, the mitzvah to love a fellow Jew is not contingent on anything other than being a member of Hashem's chosen people. (See following paragraph for exception.)

4. It is important to recognize the difference between the sin and the sinner. Despite all its statements about loving, the Torah does teach that evildoers are to be despised.[11] However, even in regard to the wicked people whom we are required to hate, the *Tanya* (ch. 32) explains that this only refers to the evil within the person. The person himself still has a spark of Godliness and is to be loved.

Furthermore, people often judge a person's character based on isolated incidents. *Tosafos (Pesachim* 113b) points out that even when it is permissible to hate certain characteristics, there is no license to harbor resentment towards the whole individual.

Chazal *(Berachos* 57a) expound on a passage in *Shir Hashirim* (4:3), "Your cheeks are like a slice of pomegranate":

---

10 Cited in *Parpara'os L'chachmah* (p. 140).
11 See *Pesachim* 113b.

even the "empty ones" (that is, the sinners of Israel) are as full of mitzvos as a pomegranate is full of seeds. Even the Jew whose actions make him seem wicked, must not be summarily dismissed. He, too, has a positive side that must be appreciated and loved.

5. We must realize that a Jew's negative attitudes may not stem from animosity to Torah. Observant Jews are often filled with righteous indignation at other people's repulsive attitudes and comments about Torah ideals and their adherents. They wonder, "Can't they see the bankruptcy of a secular value system? How can they be so spiteful as to intentionally ignore the beauty and logic of a Torah way of life?"

Unfortunately, not every person can see what may be quite obvious to others. Many people honestly think they can lead perfectly happy and fulfilling lives without changing their lifestyles. They might see that observant Jews have a better track record in producing committed Jewish children; still, it does not mean that people with other viewpoints cannot do the same. They cannot link their lack of success to their present lifestyle. Cognitive dissonance (the inability to reconcile one's intellectual awareness and actions) is a powerful force and almost everybody falls prey to it on occasion.

Even worse, it is not always the message that offends, but rather the messenger. When an Orthodox Jew presents a less than honorable image to the outside world, it affects more than the individual; the entire Torah community, and the Torah itself, is called into question. Some people, upon hearing of a Torah observant Jew, may conjure up images of a person lacking refinement. Often those who do not accept the importance of Torah study and mitzvos are only familiar with this stereotype.

Rabbi Emanuel Feldman, a prominent Orthodox rabbi from Atlanta, writes about making a hospital visit to a non-Orthodox Jew from out of state. He later received a note from the man's wife thanking him for the visit. She wrote she was pleasantly surprised to learn Orthodox rabbis visited the sick. She thought all they did was pray and study all day.

Of course there is a tremendous amount of *chesed* and kindness shown by Torah communities to their less observant brethren. Unfortunately, these acts are often overshadowed when Orthodox Jews act incorrectly or are just misunderstood.

Realizing this, we can hardly fault people for showing resentment of Torah Judaism, as hurtful as this may be. The only way to counter the resentment is by taking a genuine interest in every Jew, regardless of his or her religious leaning. This attempt can help counter misconceptions.

Only after developing a true sense of *ahavas Yisrael* can we hope to make an impact on other people's lives. Often the people most successful in Jewish outreach have not been the most charismatic or eloquent persons; rather they have been the ones to show genuine heart and feeling.

Rav Ya'akov Kaminetzky, *zt"l*, once commented on the Rambam in *Hilchos Dei'os* (6:7): One is obligated to chastise his friend (who has sinned or strayed from the proper path) over and over again, until he responds by striking out in anger. Rav Ya'akov asked (*Emes LeYa'akov, Vayetzei*), where do we ever find an exemption from a mitzvah just because one has been attacked? He explains that the mitzvah of reproof can only be fulfilled when the recipient feels it is done out of love. If he has struck out in anger, he obviously does not feel the reproof was offered out of love, so the mitzvah no longer exists.

Implementing the above suggestions could go a long way in creating a sense of unity in the Jewish community. And that may well be what is needed for the final push towards rebuilding the Beis Hamikdash speedily in our days.

Tu B'Av: Repairing the Destruction

Tu B'Av rectifies the causes of Tishah B'Av's great losses

The Talmud (*Ta'anis* 30b) describes the fifteenth day of Av as one of the two most joyous days of the year. Yom Kippur was the other. On both these days, celebrations were held in Jerusalem to enable eligible young men and women to meet, with an eye to marriage.

Six historical sources are offered for the joy of Tu B'Av:

1. On the fifteenth of Av, the Rabbis rescinded the ban on intermarriage among the tribes. When the Jews were in the desert, intermarriage was not permitted because of concerns regarding the dissolution of a tribe's property. If a woman with no brothers wed into a tribe other than her own, the land she inherited at her father's death would ultimately pass to the tribe of her husband through her children. Later, the Rabbis expounded that the prohibition regarding intermarriage applied only to the generation that first entered Canaan.

2. On the fifteenth of Av, it was determined that young women

could once again marry into the tribe of Binyamin. During the civil war between the tribe of Binyamin and the rest of the tribes (*Shoftim*, chs. 19–21), the tribes swore that that their daughters would no longer wed men from the tribe of Binyamin. On the fifteenth of Av this vow was rescinded.

3. On the fifteenth of Av, the remaining members of the generation that had left Egypt were allowed to enter the Promised Land. In the fortieth year of the Jews' trek through the desert, all of those forbidden to enter the Land had already died. Those survivors would be allowed to enter.

4. On the fifteenth of Av, the king of Israel, Hoshea ben Allah, made it possible for the ten tribes to visit Jerusalem. Earlier, the wicked Yeravam ben Nevat had installed guards to prevent members of the ten tribes from making pilgrimage to the Beis Hamikdash for the festivals. Hoshea ben Allah removed the guards.

5. On the fifteenth day of Av, the Roman decree prohibiting the burial of the Jewish dead of Betar was rescinded. Sixty years after the second Beis Hamikdash was destroyed, the great city of Betar was also leveled by the Romans, who subsequently outlawed the interment of Jewish citizens who had perished in the conflict. Years later, when the Roman law was rescinded on the fifteenth of Av, the bodies of the Jewish dead miraculously had remained intact for burial.

6. Between the beginning of the month of Nissan and the fifteenth of the month of Av, wood was chopped to be used throughout the year as fuel for the *mizbe'ach* in the Beis Hamikdas. Beginning with the fifteenth of Av, however, the days began to cool, and the wood would no longer dry properly.

Rabbeinu Gershom (*Bava Basra* 121b) comments that, relieved of this task, Jewish men had more time to study Torah.

It is not clear, however, what is so significant about these occurrences to warrant a new festival on the fifteenth of Av. Moreover, is there a common thread running through these six sources?

Perhaps if we look carefully we can see a connection between, and even a rectification of, Tishah B'Av in Tu B'Av.

The Talmud (*Ta'anis* 26b) lists five reasons for the fasting on Tishah B'Av.

1. Hashem decreed that the entire generation would not enter the Promised Land, when the spies returned from Canaan with a bad report on Tishah B'Av.

2. The first Beis Hamikdash was destroyed on the ninth of Av.

3. The second Beis Hamikdash was destroyed by the Romans on the ninth of Av.

4. The city of Betar was destroyed by the Romans on Tishah B'Av.

5. The Roman governor, Turnus Rufus, plowed up the site of the Beis Hamikdash on Tishah B'Av.

The reasons for celebration on Tu B'Av correspond to the five sources of fasting on Tishah B'Av.

1. On Tishah B'Av it was decreed that no one who had left Egypt could enter Canaan; on Tu B'Av the decree was repealed.

2. On Tishah B'Av, the first Beis Hamikdash was destroyed. According to the Talmud (*Yoma* 9a), the first Beis Hamikdash was destroyed largely because of the practice of idolatry. Elsewhere, the Talmud (*Nedarim* 81a) says that the Jews did not value Torah study properly. On Tu B'Av idolatry was countered

by the removal of Yeravam's guards. Moreover, when the people were relieved of the chore of chopping wood, they spent more time studying Torah.

3. The second Beis Hamikdash was destroyed on the ninth of Av. The Rabbis (*Yoma* 9a) cite bickering and unwarranted hatred as the cause. Presumably, this hatred was also the source of the finality of the destruction, when the site was reduced to rubble and plowed under. On Tu B'Av, peace and unity in the community were fostered by the resumption of both intertribal marriage and intermarriage with the tribe of Binyamin.

4. The city of Betar was destroyed by the Romans on Tishah B'Av; on Tu B'Av the tragedy was somewhat diminished when the Jews were finally allowed to bury their dead, and the corpses were found to have miraculously remained intact.

We should now have a better appreciation for the joy of Tu B'Av. Tishah B'Av is the saddest day of the year. When the ruptures that caused our sadness were mended on Tu B'Av, it stands to reason that the day should have happiness in equal measure.

The rectification of the repeated, historic tumult and fragmentation of the Jewish people on Tishah B'Av is beautifully countered by the building of Jewish homes in marriage. The Jewish home creates a dwelling place for Hashem's divine presence. This is what the Talmud (*Berachos* 6b) means when it says that one who rejoices with a bride and groom is considered to have rebuilt one of the ruins of Jerusalem.

May we merit once again that the glory of Hashem be revealed throughout the world.

Shabbos

The Day of the Inner Dimension

Shabbos allows us to examine our inner selves

The Torah introduces Shabbos by saying, "Hashem completed on the seventh day all of His work that He had done, and He rested from all His work that He had done" (*Bereishis* 2:2).

Rashi asks an obvious question. Hashem had already completed the Creation on the sixth day; what was left for Him to create on the seventh day? He answers that after Creation the world was still missing *menuchah*, or tranquility. Once Shabbos was established, however, tranquility came with it. Rashi implies that Shabbos is somehow connected to tranquility.

What is tranquility? And how is it related to Shabbos?

The Talmud (*Shabbos* 10b) relates that Hashem said to Moshe, "I have a precious gift for you in My treasure chest; its name is Shabbos. I want to give it to Israel; go and inform them." Why should Shabbos be more precious than any other mitzvah?

Rav Shlomo Wolbe (*Alei Shur*, vol. 2, p. 382) explains that the phrase "My treasure chest" suggests Shabbos is hidden in Hashem's "inner chambers." This means that the essence of Shabbos is focused on an inner dimension of life. In the inner dimension one can find the ultimate sense of tranquility, as mentioned in the Shabbos Minchah prayers: "A tranquility of love and generosity, a tranquility of truth and faith, a tranquility of peace and serenity, a complete tranquility that You desire...."

In one's deep, inner dimension, a person feels totally attached to and at peace with the Creator. On Shabbos, if he connects with his inner soul, he can glimpse his connection with *olam haba*, the World to Come, that inner world of the soul where all is at peace. For this reason, Shabbos is called *me'ein olam haba*, a semblance of the World to Come, because the inner focus of Shabbos is a precursor of the inner World to Come.

Shabbos and Torah study are related in that the same element of inwardness can be found in the giving of the Torah at Mount Sinai, which also occurred on Shabbos. The study of Torah is the means by which we enter the inner dimension of spirituality and holiness, because Torah itself is a *chachmah penimis*, an "inner wisdom," addressing not only the intellect, but also the soul.[1] This connection is alluded to in the Shabbos Shacharis prayers: "Moshe rejoiced in the gift of his portion, that You called him a faithful servant. A glorious crown You placed on his head when he stood before You at Mount Sinai. He brought down two stone tablets in his hand...."

It is thus important to find time to study Torah on Shabbos, especially during mealtimes, when the family is together, as this helps us focus on the inner dimensions of Shabbos.

---

1 Secular wisdom, on the other hand, is often referred to as "outside wisdom." See *Yoreh De'ah* 236:6.

The prohibition of work on Shabbos also allows us to shift our focus inward. Throughout the week our real identity is often lost, as we become one with our profession and economic standing. We overlook our soul's needs in the frenetic rat race of the workplace. When Shabbos comes, our work is done, and the focus shifts to things that are truly important, such as the soul.

We can now begin to understand the Torah's description of Shabbos as symbolic of the unique bond between Hashem and the Jewish people (*Shemos* 31:16–17):

> The Children of Israel will guard the Shabbos, to make the Shabbos an eternal covenant for their generations. Between Me and the Children of Israel it is a sign forever that in six days Hashem made heaven and earth, and on the seventh day He rested and was refreshed.

The inner dimension of Shabbos serves as a sign of the spiritually intimate relationship between Hashem and the Children of Israel.

E., a young woman studying for conversion to Judaism, once approached me. She was bothered by the Talmud's statement that a gentile is prohibited from observing the Shabbos (*Sanhedrin* 58b). Why should a gentile be forbidden to observe Shabbos more so than any other mitzvah? I gave her an example: A wealthy man would shower his wife with all types of expensive jewelry. The woman would occasionally lend her friends some of the jewelry. Most likely her husband would not mind, even if he had provided most of it. However, should the woman lend her wedding band, the husband would be quite hurt. Why the difference? The other pieces of jewelry were given as gifts; if the wife wished to share them, why should her husband mind? On the other hand, the wedding band signifies the intimate relationship between husband and wife. Anyone else wearing the ring would be intruding into the couple's relationship. Shabbos is like the wedding band. There is no harm in a gentile's observing any other mitzvah. However, the gentile's observance of Shabbos intrudes into the intimate relationship between Hashem and the Jewish people and is thus prohibited.[2]

In keeping with the above observation, we can also explain another statement in the Talmud (*Sanhedrin* 59a), which says a non-Jew may not toil in the study of Torah. Two explanations are offered: 1) the Torah is called *morashah kehillas Yaakov*, the legacy of the community of Yaakov, and not of other nations; and 2) it is called *me'orasah kehillas Yaakov*, the "betrothed" of the community of Yaakov. Why should the Torah be the exclusive legacy, or the betrothed, of the Jewish people? As stated earlier, Torah is an "inner wisdom," intimately connecting the Jewish people to Hashem. The Torah is actually compared to the "wedding ring" given by Hashem to His bride, the Jewish people.[3] As is equally true of Shabbos, the non-Jew's toiling in Torah is an intrusion into the unique relationship between Hashem and the Jewish people.

Shabbos is a day on which we recognize the inner beauty of our relationship with Hashem, His Torah, and ourselves. May we be worthy of absorbing its benefits.

---

[2] After completing this essay, I was pleased to find a similar explanation in the Midrash (*Devarim Rabbah* 1:21).

[3] Ra'avan on *Masechta Kallah Rabbasi*, p. 19, and *Machzor Vitri*, p. 336, cited by Kaplan, *Made in Heaven*.

Candle Lighting and Chava

Many of the customs associated with candle lighting serve to atone for the sin of Chava

The Shabbos is ushered in each week by the rabbinic mitzvah of lighting candles. Two reasons are cited for lighting the candles: 1) Rashi and Tosafos (Talmud, *Shabbos* 25b) understand the mitzvah as part of the general obligation to honor the Shabbos, since candlelight adds a certain elegance to the Shabbos meal; and 2) the Talmud (ibid., see Rashi) also says it is important to have light in the house, to maintain an atmosphere of *shalom bayis* (peace in the home). The Rabbis were concerned that in a dark house, people could bump into each other, thereby causing strife. The second reason requires some explanation. Although *shalom bayis* is often given a high priority, we never find Chazal ordaining a mitzvah with a *berachah* for the purpose of insuring *shalom bayis*.

Furthermore, although this mitzvah is required of every adult, there seems to be a special connection between candle lighting and the Jewish woman. It is universally accepted that the man in a Jewish household fulfills his obligation of lighting candles through his wife. Even if the husband insists on lighting the candles himself, his wife still has priority in fulfilling this mitzvah.[4] In no other mitzvah, required of both men and woman, do we find such an idea. What is the woman's connection to this mitzvah?[5]

There is also a custom associated with this mitzvah, whereby women — after candle lighting — offer special prayers and supplications to Hashem on behalf of their children. Traditionally, the candle lighting experience has provided for some of the Jewish woman's most intense moments of prayer. This practice is alluded to when the Talmud states (*Shabbos* 23b) that one who is meticulous in lighting candles will merit having children who are Torah scholars, the hope and dream of every Jewish mother. Here, too, it is not clear what the connection is between candles and children.

The Midrash (*Tanchuma* [Buber ed.], *Metzora* 17) explains that the woman lights candles to atone for the sin of Chava, the first woman. Chava brought death to the world by enticing Adam to eat from the fruit of the *eitz hada'as*, thereby extinguishing man's soul, the "light of the world" and "candle of Hashem" (*Mishlei* 20:27). Jewish women were given the opportunity to atone for Chava's sin by kindling the lights before Shabbos. We might also suggest that because Chava brought divisiveness and destruction to the home by giving her husband the fruit to eat, Jewish women were now given the mitzvah of lighting candles in the home to insure peace between herself and her husband. This

---

4 *Aruch Hashulchan* (263:7).
5 Rambam (*Hilchos Shabbos* 5:3) explains that Chazal obligated the woman to light, as she is the one who is usually home to prepare for Shabbos. However, this does not really explain the tenacity with which this mitzvah has been guarded as a woman's mitzvah.

is especially appropriate before Shabbos, the day of peace and tranquility.[6]

Now we see why the Talmud says the reward for lighting candles is good children. By kindling Shabbos candles, the woman will be worthy of creating new souls, or "candles," who will produce their own light, the light of Torah. It is, therefore, fitting for a woman to pray at that time for good children, and it is equally understandable why so many mothers of old sobbed uncontrollably at candle-lighting time.[7]

This may also be the source for the custom of adding a candle for each additional child born to the family.[8] By bringing another child into the world, the woman has "kindled another candle of Hashem," and symbolic of this accomplishment she lights another candle each week.

With the above as background, we can appreciate a rather strange custom cited by Magen Avraham (263:6). During the first week after the wife gives birth, her husband should light the candles and recite the *berachah*. The *Acharonim* try to understand the rationale for this custom.[9] Perhaps the meaning is that after a woman has brought a child into the world, she has literally "rekindled Hashem's candle." To recognize this event, she does not light the Shabbos candles during the first week; her husband does it instead.

---

6 It is interesting to note that Chava's sin also occurred on Friday afternoon, shortly before Shabbos (see *Sanhedrin* 31b).

7 A great Rav once said that the phenomenon of estranged Jews finding their way back to Torah in the most remarkable ways may very well be the fruit of a great-grandmother's tears during candle lighting.

8 Cited in *Likutei Maharich* (p. 13b).

9 See *Aruch Hashulchan* (263:7) and *Imrei Baruch* (263), who offer different explanations. This custom is generally not followed in our times. See *The Radiance of Shabbos* (Artscroll, 1986), p. 7.

Shabbos and the Mishkan

Man's rest on Shabbos endows the world with lasting holiness — as Hashem's rest gave lasting existence to the world

The fourth commandment of the *Aseres Hadibros* (*Shemos* 20:8–11) reads:

Remember the Shabbos to sanctify it. Six days you shall work and do all your labor, and the seventh day is Shabbos for Hashem your God; you shall not do any work — you, your son, your daughter, your slave, your maidservant, your animal, and your stranger within your gates. For in six days Hashem made the heavens and the earth, the sea, and all that is in them, and He rested on the seventh day. Therefore, Hashem blessed the seventh day and sanctified it.

These passages imply we observe the Shabbos and do not perform any work on it, to commemorate Hashem's creation of the world and His having rested on the seventh day. However, this understanding requires further explanation. First, what is meant when it says that Hashem "rested" on Shabbos? Hashem's creation of heaven and earth during the first six days did not involve any effort requiring rest afterwards.[10] And second, how does our not working on Shabbos show anything about Hashem's creation during the first six days?

The *Ohr Hachaim* (*Bereishis* 2:2) understands the concept of Hashem's "resting" to mean that everything created was not yet firmly established — until Shabbos. On Shabbos Hashem endowed the world with its own "life-force," thereby giving it lasting existence.[11] Thus Hashem's "rest" means He allowed the world to become more settled, or "rested." But we must still explain how Hashem's rest is connected with our resting on Shabbos.

Rav Samson Raphael Hirsch (*Shemos* 20:10–11) offers a beautiful interpretation of the prohibited activities on Shabbos. He explains that it has nothing to do with resting from hard labor. Rather, when man refrains from creative labor on Shabbos, he acknowledges Hashem's total mastery over Creation. Man can do nothing — not even flicking a light switch or picking a flower — without the permission and assistance of the Master Creator. But, again, this has nothing to do with Hashem's "resting" on the seventh day.

We can explain by using an insight from Rabbi Yitzchak Noble in his *sefer Imrei Yitzchak*. The Talmud derives the laws of

---

10 Indeed, Rashi (*Shemos* 20:11) explains that the Torah employs the expression "Hashem rested" to teach man that he too must rest after his work days. But this also needs explanation, for if the concept of rest does not exist in regard to Hashem, how are we emulating Him?

11 The Ohr Hachaim says this is what the torah means by "*Uvayom hashvi'i shavas vayinafash*" — "On the seventh day He rested and was refreshed" (*Shemos* 31:17). "*Vayinafash*," refreshed, comes from the word "*nefesh*," or soul, meaning that Hashem endowed the world with its soul.

Shabbos from the construction of the *mishkan*. Thirty-nine different types of labor were employed in the construction of the *mishkan*, and these thirty-nine categories form the basis of prohibited activities on Shabbos. What is the connection between Shabbos and the *mishkan*? Rabbi Noble explains that the *mishkan* was built to create a repository for Hashem's divine presence (*Shemos Rabbah* 34:1). In the same manner that Hashem created the world as a dwelling place for man, He also wanted man to create a *mishkan*, a microcosm of the world, wherein His divine presence would reside.[12] And just as Hashem "rested" on the seventh day in order to give His creation lasting substance, He wanted man, too, to rest on the seventh day from creating the *mishkan*, in order to endow it with lasting holiness.

This explains why the construction of the *mishkan* was halted on Shabbos, while the sacrifices were offered on Shabbos, too. The Jewish people's relationship to the *mishkan* closely mirrored Hashem's activity in the world. As Hashem ceased to create on Shabbos while continuing to maintain the world, so man was prohibited from building the *mishkan* on Shabbos, although he was obligated to maintain the sacrificial order.

We can now understand why the categories of prohibited labor on Shabbos are derived from the *mishkan*. By refraining from activities involved in building the *mishkan*, we emulate, in some small way, Hashem's rest after creating the world. Furthermore, Hashem's "rest" was followed by His blessing the Shabbos and sanctifying it, as seen in the passage quoted earlier. Rashi ex-

---

12 The Talmud (*Berachos* 55a) says Betzalel, the architect of the *mishkan*, understood the "combinations of letters" that Hashem used in creating the universe. The *Midrash Tanchuma* (*Pekudei* 2) finds many parallels between the building of the *mishkan* and the creation of the universe.

plains Hashem's blessing as referring to the double portion of manna that fell for Shabbos when the Jews were in the desert. We, too, emulate Hashem's blessing and sanctification when we recite the Kiddush and the *berachah* on the two loaves of bread.

The observance of Shabbos thus gives substance to our belief in Hashem's having created the world, as it emulates His creation and "rest," by commemorating our own creation and rest while constructing the *mishkan*, the microcosm of the world.

The Shabbos Family

The Shabbos experience promotes harmony in the family

I recently participated in a panel discussion for health care workers on the topic of cultural sensitivity. My presentation, "The Orthodox Jewish Patient's Needs," followed similar discussions of "Amish Health Care" and "The Medical Beliefs of J-'s Witnesses." After each speaker's presentation the floor was opened to questions and comments.

I had finished my talk and had fielded about a half-dozen questions, when a nurse raised her hand. She meekly inquired whether she could ask a question unrelated to my talk. I agreed, though I was a little uneasy about what to expect. She explained that she worked at a clinic to which many Orthodox families brought their children. She then asked, "How do your people get their children to behave so nicely?"

At first I was shocked. The woman who had asked the question obviously had seen a marked difference in the behavior of Orthodox Jewish children. What explanation could I offer to this largely gentile audience? On impulse, I asked the group, "How many times a month do any of you have a meal with your whole family — a meal uninterrupted by phone calls, business appointments, computer games, or television?" Not one of the sixty or seventy people in the audience raised a hand.

"The Jewish family," I said, "is guaranteed two such meals a week: Friday night and Saturday lunch. We don't answer or make phone calls, we don't engage in any type of business activities, and we don't play computer games, or turn on the television. The children don't get driven to the houses of friends or to sports activities, because we do not drive cars for that twenty-five-hour period. We don't even drive to play tennis or golf. The family has no choice but to sit together at a festive table and actually talk with each other! This special time helps us develop close relationships and allows for a foundation of greater parental authority."

Part of the purpose of the Shabbos experience is to strengthen the family ties. Shabbos is first introduced in the Torah in the *Aseres Hadibros* (*Shemos* 20:10) with the following words: "Remember the Shabbos to sanctify it. Six days you shall work and do all your labor, and the seventh day is Shabbos for Hashem your God; you shall not do any work — you, your son, [and] your daughter..." (*Shemos* 20:8–10).

Why does the Torah mention the obligation of one's children to observe the Shabbos? Why should we think that one's children would *not* be obligated to observe the laws of Shabbos? The Mechilta explains that the Torah refers to minor children who are generally not obligated in the observance of mitzvos. But, if so, why is it that the responsibility to sanctify the Shabbos is greater than any other mitzvah? We may suggest that the Torah recognizes Shabbos as a time of family sharing. Shabbos is intimately connected with the family. The shared experience of family members, even young children, is the foundation of the Jewish family and the Jewish community.

Similarly, the Torah introduces the mitzvah of respecting one's parents in the same sentence as the mitzvah of observing Shabbos: "Your mother and father shall you revere and My Shabbos shall you observe" (*Vayikra* 19:3).

The Talmud (*Yevamos* 6a) derives from this juxtaposition that if a parent instructs a child to violate the laws of Shabbos, the child must not obey. Clearly, if the child is put in the position of having to disregard the parent's wishes, the child cannot revere the parent. The linking of the two mitzvos suggests that observance of Shabbos is a prerequisite for parental respect. Thus, the Torah seems to suggest that proper observance of Shabbos is essential to the appropriate bond between parent and child.

This may give us a deeper understanding of the lighting of candles before Shabbos. The Talmud (*Shabbos* 25b) explains that we light candles to create an atmosphere of *shalom bayis*. This is especially important at the Shabbos table, where fostering a peaceful relationship among family members is an essential element of the meal. Mothers pray for their children's welfare after lighting the candles. Fathers bless their children when they return home from the synagogue. Shabbos is the time when our relationships with our children are deepened.

The emphasis on peace allows us to more fully grasp another custom. The Talmud (*Shabbos* 119b) relates that two angels escort a person home from the synagogue on Friday evening. One of the angels is good, the other is evil. On arriving home, if the person finds the table set and the candles lit in honor of Shabbos, the good angel blesses the home. The evil angel must answer "Amen." If, however, the house has not been prepared for

Shabbos, the evil angel curses the home, and the good angel must answer "Amen." Based on this narrative from the Talmud, at the beginning of the meal it is customary to sing *Shalom Aleichem*: "Peace to you, ministering angels!... Come in peace, O angels of peace.... Bless us with peace, O angels of peace."

Why are the angels referred to as "angels of peace"? And why do we ask them to bless us with peace rather than any other blessing? The focus of the Shabbos table is creating peaceful harmony in the home. Hashem sends His special messengers of peace to bless our homes on Shabbos. May we merit the blessings of a blessed and peaceful Shabbos!

Glossary

Acharonim — The later commentators, from the period beginning in the latter part of the fifteenth century.

ahavas Yisrael — The mitzvah to love a fellow Jew.

akeidah — The binding of Isaac, referring to the challenge given our forefather Abraham to offer his son Isaac as a sacrifice.

aliyah — The honor of being called to the Torah.

Amalek — A nation who descended from Esau and became the archenemies of Hashem and the Jewish people. There is a mitzvah to wipe out the memory of Amalek.

Amidah — The silent prayer of devotion recited three times each day, four times on Shabbos and holidays.

arayos — The prohibited marital relationships.

Asarah B'Teves — The tenth day of Teves, a fast day commemorating the siege on Jerusalem.

Aseres Hadibros — The Decalogue, consisting of the Ten Commandments that Moshe heard directly from God and then transcribed on two stone tablets.

bein — Between.

beis din — The Jewish court.

Beis Hamikdash (pl. *Batei Mikdash*) — The Holy Temple in Jerusalem. There were two Temples: the first was destroyed in 422 BCE, and the second was destroyed in 68 CE.

berachah — A blessing.

binah — A depth of understanding.

chachamim — Torah scholars.

Chashmonaim — The family of *kohanim* who led the war against the Greeks in the Chanukah story.

Chazal — The Sages from Talmudic and pre-Talmudic times.

chesed — Acts of loving-kindness.

chok (pl. *chukim*) — The group of mitzvos without any logical explanation for their observance.

chuppah — The marriage canopy.

dreidel — A four-sided toy top used during Chanukah; the letters *nun, gimmel, heh,* and *shin* are written on it, on each side.

eigel — The golden calf that the Jews made at Mount Sinai.

eitz hada'as — The Tree of Knowledge in the Garden of Eden.

Eretz Yisrael — The Land of Israel.

galus — exile; usually used in reference to the Jewish exile since the Temple's destruction.

Havdalah — The prayer recited upon the departure of Shabbos, marking the separation between Shabbos and the week.

Hoshana Rabbah — The seventh day of Sukkos, considered to be the last day of judgment in the High Holiday season.

kedushah — Holiness.

Kiddush — The prayer of sanctification, recited over a cup of wine on Shabbos and holidays.

Lag Ba'omer — A holiday marking the thirty-third day of the omer.

lechem oni — Bread of affliction, a reference to matzo.

lishmah — The fulfillment of mitzvos for the sole purpose of serving God, without any ulterior motive or gain.

ma'aser (pl. *ma'aseros*) — A tithe taken from produce grown in Eretz Yisrael and given to the *levi*.

malchiyos — The section in the Rosh Hashanah Musaf *Amidah* that tells of God's mastery of the world.

matanos l'evyonim — The special mitzvah to distribute charity on Purim.

middos — Character traits.

Midrash — A collection of traditions and interpretations of the biblical narratives written by the authors of the Mishnah.

mishkan — The Tabernacle built by the Jews in the Sinai Desert as a place to serve God. The *mishkan* served this function for almost five hundred years, until the Temple was built by King Solomon.

mishlo'ach manos — The mitzvah to deliver food gifts to one's friends on Purim.

Minchah — The daily afternoon prayer.

mizbe'ach — The altar upon which sacrifices were brought.

mo'ed (pl. *mo'adim*) — Jewish holiday(s).

motza'ei Shabbos — The night folloiwng Shabbos, Saturday night.

Musaf — The additional *Amidah* prayer recited on Shabbos and holidays.

neder, (pl. *nedarim*) — Vow(s), usually of abstinence from some physical pleasure.

na'aseh v'nishma — Lit. "We will do and we will listen," the Jewish people's response to Hashem's offering them the Torah.

nes niglah — An overt miracle.

nes nistar — A hidden miracle that is masked by nature.

Parashas Hachodesh — The Shabbos before, or on, Rosh Chodesh Nissan.

Parashas Parah — The first or second Shabbos after Purim, commemorating the red heifer used in the purification process during the times of the Temple.

Parashas Shekalim — The Shabbos before, or on, Rosh Chodesh Adar, commemorating the half-shekel tax collected during the times of the Temple.

Parashas Zachor — The Shabbos before Purim, commemorating the war against Amalek.

Rishonim — The "early" commentators, spanning the period between the eleventh and fifteenth centuries.

sefiras ha'omer — Lit. the counting of the omer offering, referring to the seven weeks between the omer offering brought in the Temple on the second day of Pesach, and Shavuos.

selichos — The special prayers recited early in the morning, before Rosh Hashanah and during the the Ten Days of Repentance.

Shacharis — The daily morning prayer.

shalom bayis — Domestic peace.

Shemini Atzeres — The eighth day of Sukkos, considered to be a holiday by itself.

shevuah — An oath.

Shiv'ah Asar B'Tamuz — The seventeenth day of Tamuz, a fast day commemorating the breaching of the walls of Jerusalem.

shofaros — The section of the Rosh Hashanah Musaf *Amidah* that discusses the meaning of the shofar.

shtei halechem — The offering of two wheat loaves brought in the Beis Hamikdash on Shavuos.

sinas chinam — Unwarranted hatred.

temurah — The prohibition of switching the sanctity of one animal to another.

Ta'anis Esther — The fast day on the thirteenth day of Adar.

Tachanun — A prayer of supplication that is recited daily after the morning and afternoon *Amidah*, except on Jewish holidays and at special occasions, such as a circumcision or wedding.

taharah — Ritual purity.

terumah (pl. *terumos*) — A tithe taken from produce grown in Eretz Yisrael and given to the *kohen*.

teshuvah — Lit. return, referring to the act of repentance from sin.

Tishah B'Av — The ninth day of Av, a day of mourning for the loss of the two Temples in Jerusalem.

Tu B'Av — The fifteenth day of Av, a holiday celebrating different occasions in Jewish history.

Tu B'Shevat — The fifteenth day of Shevat, the New Year for Trees.

tumah — Ritual impurity.

tumas meis — The ritual impurity imparted by either direct contact with a corpse, or when under the same roof or covering as the corpse; *tamei meis* is the person who becomes defiled.

tzelem Elokim — The image of God.

Tzom Gedalia — A fast on the third day of Tishrei, commemorating the assassination of Gedalia, the Jewish governor of Israel, following the destruction of the first Beis Hamikdash.

tzorres — Troubles.

vidui — Confession prayer recited on Yom Kippur.

yahrzeit — The anniversary of a person's death.

Yamim Noraim — Days of Awe, referring to the High Holiday season.

Yerushalmi — Jerusalem Talmud.

yetzer hara — The evil inclination that tries to lead a person to sin.

yibum — The mitzvah for a man to marry his deceased and childless brother's widow.

zichronos — The section of the Rosh Hashanah Musaf *Amidah* that evokes God's remembering the Jewish people's merits.

לזכרון עולם בהיכל ה'
מוקדש לעלוי נשמת אבי מורי
חיים בן דוד
Herbert Harris MD

ולנשמות דודי ודודתי
יעקב בן אברהם
ושרה בת דוד
Jack and Sylvia Rotner

Whose integrity, kindness, and generosity were truly remarkable. They remain a source of inspiration and strength. May the dedication of this book serve as an elevation for their souls.

Moshe and Sydney Harris and family

לזכר נשמות
אמו אלטע מינדל בת אליהו הכהן
אביה דוב זאב בן יצחק מאיר
דודה יחזקאל בן חיים הכהן
אחיו משה יצחק בן אהרן

by Edward and Iris Moskowitz

In loving memory of
Dr. Leo Dworkin
אליהו בן אברהם

by his wife Alva
daughter Dr. Deborah Ross
son Dr. Jeffrey Dworkin

לזכרון עולם
מארישע בת ישעיה הכהן
יצחק בן ישעיה הכהן
משה בן אברהם

In loving memory of
Rose Stein
רייזל בת מאיר

by Irwin and Lorna Shulman and family

לע"נ
האי גברא שנתנסה ביסורין רבים ועמד בכולם
גדליה לייב בן הירש מאטיל ע"ה

לזכר נשמת
ישראל שמאי בן
משה הכהן זימברג ז"ל

In loving memory of
Stanley Muszynski
ישראל בן דוד

Stanley Yulish
שלמה בן ישראל

Ina Yulish
אסתר חיה בת משה

Minna and Isadore Yulish
Murray Eskin
Zelda and David Muszynski
Lea and Izrael Lew

May this dedication serve in their merit.
Susan, Stanley, Sarah, and Steven
Muszynski